NATURAL EVANGELISM
WITH NO ARTIFICIAL INGREDIENTS

NATURAL EVANGELISM

WITH NO

ARTIFICIAL

INGREDIENTS

J. JOHN

Text copyright © 1996 Lynx Communications
and Anglican Renewal Ministries

Text by J. John
Adapted for this edition by Frances Grant

Published by
Lynx Communications
Sandy Lane West, Oxford OX4 5HG, England
ISBN UK 0 7459 3389 0

Albatross Books Pty Ltd
PO Box 320, Sutherland, NSW 2232, Australia
ISBN Australia 0 7324 1356 7

First edition 1996
10 9 8 7 6 5 4 3 2 1 0

A catalogue for this book is available from the British Library
Printed and bound in Great Britain

Acknowledgments

Every effort has been made to trace and contact copyright
owners. If there are any inadvertent ommissions in the
acknowledgments, we apologize to those concerned and will
remedy these in the next edition.

Scripture quotations taken from the Holy Bible, New
International Version. Copyright © 1973,1978,1984 by
International Bible Society. Used by permission of Hodder and
Stoughton Limited, a member of the Hodder Headline plc
Group. All rights reserved.

The story of Mrs Smith from *Urban Perspectives* by Dr Robert
Lupton.
The Revd Marie Elizabeth Dyer quoted in *The Task of the
Whole Church* by John B. Coburn.

Contents

Introduction

Someone once asked me what my churchmanship was.
What a question! I said, 'I'm a Catholic, charismatic,
evangelical,' and they said, 'What's that?! Is *that a
Christian*?!'

I don't know why we have to attach such labels to
ourselves—I hope it's not pomposity. Rather, I hope
that it's to say one thing above all others—that I want,
passionately, to *tell* people the good news about Jesus
Christ.

And just in case you're thinking, 'Well it's easy for
him, he does it for a living...,' let me tell you that I
find it as hard as anyone. For instance, my wife and I
once had one of those absolutely textbook disputes
with a neighbour—you know, about whose fence it
is—and after trying to unravel the rights and wrongs of
it all, and failing, we tried to do the Christian thing by
paying for it even though we thought it wasn't our
fence. Sounds good, doesn't it? But *then* when we
went out into the garden, everyone was embarrassed
and didn't want to talk. And I thought, hey... here am I
meant to be telling them all about the gospel, but it's
not that easy, is it? It's not that easy at all.

This book has been written for one simple, but
paradoxical, reason. I honestly believe, despite what
I've just said, that the secret of successful evangelism
lies in our being *natural* about it, in just being our
normal, ordinary selves; but I also know that it's hard.

For those who can accept both sides of this coin, then this course is for you. Few of us are truly gifted on the soapbox, and then there's stress, which makes things even worse. The answer, for those who want to evangelize but aren't sure how, is to be found simply in being ordinary—sharing a joke, a story, a problem, an anecdote, in the normal run of the daily minutiae of our lives. We meet people throughout our day with whom we are our natural selves; and we can be natural for God.

So, welcome to *Natural Evangelism—With No Artificial Ingredients*! I hope that as a guide it will provide you with:

◆ a course in personal evangelism;

◆ exercises to help you sharpen your skills, at the end of the main body of each chapter;

◆ daily studies for private meditation and prayer.

You may already have taken part in the video course for groups, called *Saints in Evangelism*, at church, perhaps, or in a house fellowship. If you have, then this book will help to confirm the work you did on that course.

But this book is also designed to take you through the work, from scratch, at a more personal level. This way, you can grow in evangelism skills at your own pace and in your own time, with the gifts and talents that are natural to you as an individual.

Exercises, notebooks and bookmarks!

What are your hopes as you approach this course? Throughout this book, and especially in the exercises that come at the end of each chapter, you will be invited to record some of your thoughts, and your growing understanding of what God wants you to do. Buy yourself a simple jotter, roughly two-thirds A4 size (an A4 pad would be too big), with blank pages rather than ruled lines; your local stationer will almost certainly have them. Make this your own personal workbook—you will be amazed later at how many important things you have written!

This book also frequently suggests that you put it down and do something else! Have to hand a block of those small, yellow, low-tack paper markers, so that you can find your place again. Whenever you have to stop, line up a marker with the sentence you have just finished, so that you can continue later with the minimum interruption to the flow of your thoughts.

Daily studies

The aim throughout this course is that you will learn much and travel a long way in natural evangelism. In order to understand how to use the Daily Studies, have a Bible to hand—you will need one throughout the book. Have your notebook ready as well, and use it to write down passages that seem to speak to you personally.

Before you begin, spend some moments in prayer, committing this important journey to the Lord. Invite the Holy Spirit to come and work in your life, so that by the end of the course you will be equipped and enthused to spread the good news of Jesus to your friends and neighbours.

Finally, in all sincerity may I wish you success in your work. It's not always easy, so relax: be normal and natural and you're half way there. Go for it!

CHAPTER 1

Why evangelize?

That's a very good question, and before it can be answered there's even a problem about the very word itself—'evangelism'—as demonstrated by the following story:

> *About a century ago, there was a meeting of a group of elders in a homely little church, in northern England. They were talking about the latest motion that someone had put forward, which was about getting another chandelier for the church.*
>
> *The motion had been read out, and everyone had sat around for a bit, mumbling, and humming and haa-ing, until one of the elders began with an objection to it.*
>
> *'I don't know,' he said, 'but I don't really see why we need one of these. Most of our congregation won't even be able to spell the silly thing, let alone get anything out of it.'*
>
> *'I agree,' said the next elder. 'And anyway, we've just got a new pipe organ. The last thing we need is another musical instrument.'*
>
> *'Absolutely,' said a third. 'What this church actually needs is better lighting!'*

So let's be clear about what we really mean by the term evangelism. In reality, it's no more and no less than this:

Evangelism is one beggar telling another beggar where to find bread.

Charles Spurgeon

To put it a bit more formally, The Anglican Archbishops Consultation in Cyprus in 1989 worded it this way:

To evangelize is to make known by word and deed the love of the crucified and risen Christ in the power of the Holy Spirit, so that people will repent, believe and receive Christ as their Saviour and obediently serve him as their Lord in the fellowship of his Church.

In the New Testament, the verb 'to evangelize' is used fifty-two times. Its meaning is 'to declare, proclaim, announce or state good news'. In Luke 4:18 we find Jesus in the synagogue reading from Isaiah chapter 61:

The Spirit of the Lord is on me, because he has anointed me to preach good news to the poor. He has sent me to proclaim freedom for the prisoners and recovery of sight for the blind, to release the oppressed, to proclaim the year of the Lord's favour.

In other words, Jesus' ministry was to evangelize. It is clear from this and from the life and ministry of Jesus that one side of the coin is the proclamation of the good news (words), and that the other side is the demonstration of the good news (works and wonders).

Evangelism in its biblical sense is concerned with individuals and their relationship to God, and also their relationship and responsibility to others. Service,

11

worship, education, pastoral care and evangelism are bound together in the one mission. The mission of the Church is to restore all people to unity with God and each other in Christ.

Why should we evangelize at all?

To begin with, the answer to this question lies in the fact that the Bible commands it. In many ways, this is the strongest and arguably the most important of all reasons. It is both God's Word and God's will.

The Great Commission

There are clear instructions from Jesus in the Gospels to spread the good news. Jesus has given his church a mandate to 'go and make disciples'. This has become known as the Great Commission:

> *Therefore go and make disciples of all nations, baptizing them in the name of the Father and of the Son and of the Holy Spirit and teaching them to obey everything I have commanded you. And surely I am with you, always, to the very end of the age.*
>
> Matthew 28:19–20

The command has three important parts:

◆ Make disciples; people need to become committed to Jesus Christ.

◆ Mark disciples, 'baptizing them in the name of the

Father, of the Son and of the Holy Spirit.' If people haven't been baptized, they need to become so; and if they have then they need to be identified as Christians.

◆ Mature disciples; 'teach them to obey everything I have commanded you.' Jesus' teaching needs to be taught and applied.

Note here that the process has to include each of the three parts. It's not 'make and mark'; it's not 'make and mature'; and it's not 'mark and mature'; it is 'make, mark and mature'.

Other important reasons

There are, however, many other reasons for evangelizing, and all of them are positive ones. The Bible is not some unwelcome, Dickensian rule-book that we are obliged to oppress others with (if it ever was). To the contrary, those who have committed their lives to Jesus have enormous enthusiasm for the Bible as a work of great freedom and light, of love and social justice. Naturally enough, this enthusiasm is contagious, but it does more than just 'catch on': it also enables people to strive for more peaceful, healthy and loving lives. Evangelism is not just a passion passed from one to another; it is also good for one and all.

◆ **... because of people's needs**

If we really love God, we will love people. Jesus evangelized because of the depth of compassion in his heart for people who were like sheep without a shepherd (Matthew 9:36–38).

◆ ... because Jesus believed in evangelism

If we really love Jesus we will love other people. We live in a world that has grown callous to other people's needs. Jesus certainly wasn't callous—human needs moved him. When he saw the crowds, he had compassion on them because they were harassed and helpless, like sheep without a shepherd.

Nor was his compassion some sort of lofty intellectual exercise. He really, *really* cared. For instance, say that your family has been out walking in the forest one day and at some point you realize you've lost one of the two children. Would you say, 'Oh well, never mind, we had two and now we've only got one.'? Or, 'Cheer up dear, half a loaf is better than none.'? You bet your life you wouldn't! You'd call and search and call again and search on further until you found your lost child, alive or dead. You'd be desperate to find the lost one. And *that's* how Jesus feels and cares about the lost, the wandering, the hungry and the fearful.

◆ ... because compassion is all-important

There is a significant difference between pity and compassion. Pity says, in effect, 'Oh dear, what a shame. How sad,' and does nothing. But compassion says, 'I simply cannot let it happen,' and acts.

More than anyone who has ever lived, Jesus had compassion. The original Greek translated compassion as a very strong word, full of deep gut level feeling and emotion. It is being moved to the depths of one's heart. The Latin word from which we get our English word 'compassion' means 'suffering with someone'— entering into the depths of their despair and pain.

The importance of compassion and action in the communication of the Christian faith cannot be over-emphasized. Compassion works for evangelism because there is an element of suffering in it, and suffering is what makes the church authentic.

◆ ... because the early church believed in evangelism

Concern for people led Jesus to long for more labourers:

> *The harvest is plentiful, but the workers are few. Ask the Lord of the harvest, therefore, to send out workers into the harvest field.*
> **Matthew 9:36–38**

All living things grow. Jesus, too, was committed to the growth of what he saw as a living organism—his church. He said: '... I will build my church' (Matthew 16:18), and wherever he went he proclaimed the good news of the kingdom of God, backing up his preaching with demonstrations of the power and love of God (Mark 1:32–34).

'Building' is a term that clearly implies development and expansion. It still is Jesus' church and he still does want it to grow. When we look at many of the parables of Jesus we find he used growth terminology and imagery. Many of his parables were drawn from farming—an occupation obviously concerned with growth!

15

It is also clear that after Jesus' death and resurrection the first Christians, too, believed in growth. The church in Jerusalem grew from 120 to many thousands, as the book of Acts tells us:

◆ *Acts 1:15: In those days Peter stood up among the believers—a group numbering 120.*

◆ *Acts 2:41: Those who accepted his message were baptized and about 3,000 were added to their number that day.*

◆ *Acts 2:47: The Lord added to their number daily (that is, 365 new Christians at least each year!).*

◆ *Acts 3:4: Many who heard the message believed, and the number grew to 5,000.*

◆ *Acts 5:14: More and more men and women believed in the Lord and were added to their number.*

◆ *Acts 6:7: The Word of God spread and a large number of priests became obedient to the faith.*

◆ *Acts 21:20: You see... how many thousands of Jews have believed. (Approximately twenty-five years later in AD59.)*

The city of Jerusalem had a population of about 250,000 people, but the church grew from its beginning (about 120 people) to such large numbers that the high priest said, 'You have filled Jerusalem with your teaching!' (Acts 5:28). Tremendous growth was the norm in the New Testament church.

◆ **... because the fulfilment of prophecy demands evangelism**

Jesus said: 'The gospel of the kingdom will be preached in the whole world as a testimony to all nations, and then the end will come' (Matthew 24:14).

Jesus is saying that one of the prerequisites to his return is the spread of the Christian message to the whole world. Note, however, that the Bible does not say that there will be world conversion before Jesus returns; it simply says there will be world evangelism. Everyone must hear, although not everyone will respond.

The task that Jesus gave to his church to preach the gospel to every nation is getting larger every day, with the growth in world population. The world population at the time of Jesus was about 170 million. In 1995, it was about 5,500 million, and by the year 2000 the world population is projected to be around 6,200 million. There are 218 nations and 5,000 languages—and everyone must hear the good news!

◆ ... a pleasure not a pain

If evangelism is merely one's job rather than one's joy we will soon get stale. Let this story cheer us on:

A Christian family were on holiday travelling down a road when they saw a suitcase fly off the top of a car going in the opposite direction. They stopped to pick it up, but the driver of the other car never stopped. The only clue to the driver's identity was a gold coin with the inscription, 'Given to Otis Sampson on his retirement by Portland Cement Company'.

After an extensive correspondence, Otis Sampson was located and contacted. He wrote a letter telling them to discard the suitcase and

*contents and send only the gold coin. Mr
Sampson used the phrase 'my most precious
possession' several times to describe the gold
coin. They sent the gold coin with a letter about
their most prized possession—Jesus Christ.*

*A year later they received a Christmas package.
In it was the gold coin. Mr Sampson wrote: 'You
will be happy to know we have become Christians
and active members of a church. We want you to
have this gold coin. I am seventy-four and my
wife is seventy-two. You were the first people to
tell us about Jesus. Now he is our most prized
possession.*

What do I mean by artificial ingredients? Well, there are
the obvious ones like dress—no one needs to dress a
certain way (or wear a dog-collar!) to be a Christian,
on Sunday or any other day. Then there are certain
rituals that can be deeply significant for those who
understand them but pretty useless for those who
don't, such as lighting special candles and burning
incense, or not eating meat on certain days. And then
there are subtler ingredients, such as exclusive phrases
and jargon which basically imply 'holier-than-thou'. Do
these things help to draw people to God or distance
them even more?

... because the majority of churches believe this should be a Decade of Evangelism

It is now officially recognized that evangelism is the
primary task given to the church:

This conference, recognizing that evangelism is the primary task given to the church, asks each Province and Diocese of the Anglican Communion, in cooperation with other Christians, to become committed to making the closing ten years of this millennium a Decade of Evangelism with a renewed and united emphasis on making Christ known to the people of this world .

Resolution 43 of the 1988 Lambeth Conference

But why me?

Christians are like Arctic rivers: frozen at the mouth!

Wilson Carlile, founder of the Church Army

Despite all the reasons we have seen at the start of this chapter, it is very much easier to understand why people *don't* evangelize, rather than why they do. There are all sorts of reasons, usually based on fear; as a result, as someone once said, 'Christianity is one of the best kept secrets in the church.'

Recognizing fear

Does the word 'evangelism' strike you with fear and alarm? Do you break out in a sweat? Do you feel a cold draught at the thought of sharing *your* Christian faith with other people?

Fear is nothing new. It is several thousand years since the following proverb was written: 'Fear of other people will prove to be a snare' (Proverbs 29:25). Even then, it was recognized that our biggest fear—of other people—is the one which, more than anything else, causes the feeling of being trapped and stuck, unable to get out.

Nor is it enough glibly to quote that 'perfect love casts out fear'! That's far easier said than done! There have been times when I have felt confused and frustrated at this and many other Bible verses to 'fear not'. It would be more true to say that 'fear casts out our perfect love!'

Let us take a look at some of these fears. For example, 'I don't know what to say'; 'I may not be able to answer their questions'; 'I'm afraid I might do more harm than good'.

In fact, the beginning of finding a solution to fear comes with some of the most simple assurances to be found in the Bible. As the apostle Paul writes in 1 Corinthians 2:1, 'As for me, when I came to you it was not with any show of oratory or philosophy, but *simply* to tell you what God has guaranteed.'

When we study the ministry of Jesus we find that he taught profound truths in very simple ways. Why do so many people think we should do the exact opposite— teach simple truths in profound ways! Jesus said, 'Unless you change and become like little children, you will never enter the kingdom of heaven' (Matthew 18:3).

My children are always asking questions! But to be scared of them is hardly the answer. If they ask me questions I haven't got a clue about, I tell them I'll either think about the question or ask a friend. (It's amazing how they remind me for the answer! 'Dad, you said you'd find out what God does all day—what does he do?' 'Dad, can Jesus come for lunch?')

Fear of inadequacy

Take, for instance, the fear of being inadequate. We may be concerned about what we do not know. But is what we do not know really of primary importance? Instead, surely we should share what we *do* know? Each and every one of us has a unique store of experience and understanding, and it is this which we are called upon to be confident enough to share with others.

Of course, we are still quite free to say, 'I don't know' to people's questions. But at the same time, when we do come across questions that we don't know the answer to, we should also be prepared to go and do some homework.

Fear of losing our reputation

We are so often very concerned about what others will think of us. 'I'll get labelled a Bible-basher'; 'They'll think I'm a religious nut-case!' But what did Jesus say about this? His example is summed up in Philippians:

> *He made himself nothing.*
> **Philippians 2:7**

So that when Jesus was crucified *he had no reputation to lose*. It is essential that we find our affirmation from Jesus and, as the verse in Philippians goes on to say, take 'the very nature of a servant'. The apostle Paul gives us the model of the soldier who 'wants to please his commanding officer' (2 Timothy 2:4). It is Jesus we are serving and trying to please.

If we are to be serious about evangelizing, we must be prepared to be servants, not teachers. We must not worry about being thought unusual, or even odd, and we must accept in advance that, to some who are not Christians, the Christian message can sound downright foolish:

> *For the message of the cross is foolishness to those who are perishing.*
> **1 Corinthians 1:18**

However, wisdom and foolishness are only the light and shadow of the same candle, as the following two stories demonstrate. The first concerns a man called Richard Wurmbrandt, who was imprisoned in various government prisons because of his Christian activities. In one account, he wrote this:

> *A number of us decided to pay the price for the privilege of preaching. So we accepted the terms, it was a deal. We preached, they beat us. We were happy preaching, they were happy beating us. We were all happy.*

But I wonder who were the ultimate winners in this situation? I'm pretty sure it wasn't the jailers.

The second story is that of the forty martyrs of Sebaste. It goes like this:

> *It was in the middle of a very bitter winter, in the year AD320. There were forty soldiers, all Christians, who were just a few members of the famed Twelfth Legion of Rome's imperial army. One day their captain told them that Emperor*

Licinius had sent out an edict that all soldiers were to offer sacrifices to the pagan gods.

Most of the army dutifully obeyed, but the Christians did not. Instead, their response was, 'You can have our armour and even our bodies, but our hearts' allegiance belongs to Jesus Christ.'

At this, the captain had them marched onto a nearby frozen lake. He had them stripped of their clothes and said they must either die or renounce Christ. But they would not. Instead, these brave people sang Christian songs together throughout the night and, one by one, they fell to the ice as the temperature took its toll. At last there was only one soldier left. Finally, this last person lost his courage and he stumbled to the shore, where he did, indeed, renounce Christ.

But an officer of the guards had been watching all this, and unknown to the others he had secretly come himself to believe in Christ. When he saw this last man break rank he could keep his secret no longer. He walked out onto the ice, threw off his clothes, and confessed that he also was a Christian. When the sun rose the next morning, there were again forty bodies of soldiers who had fought to the death for Christ.

Doesn't our fear of losing reputation seem trifling when compared to some of our brothers and sisters who have lost lives and literally feared physical harm when they stood for Jesus Christ? When we think of the lives of the great martyrs, from Stephen in the first century AD to Martin Luther King just a few decades ago, is our reputation really so precious?

What we must learn is how not to be offended, how not to take people's adverse comments personally. (Of course we must not be foolish in the way we share the message, but that's a different issue: that's a matter of being sensitive, so that we don't get in the way of the message—more of that in Chapter 4.)

Fear of rejection

None of us likes to be rejected. Rejection is very hard to handle, since we have a built-in need for love and acceptance. In evangelism, we can often find some people to be neither loving nor accepting.

The Bible tells us that right at the start of his ministry, Jesus experienced rejection.

> *He came to that which was his own, but his own did not receive him.*
>
> John 1:11

> *Jesus himself made it clear that if we are going to follow him we should not be surprised that some will reject us. After all, he was 'despised and rejected by men'.*
>
> Isaiah 53:3

> *They got up, drove him out of the town, and took him to the brow of a hill in order to throw him down the cliff.*
>
> Luke 4:29

The Greek word for witness is *marturia* and it is from this that we derive the English word, 'martyr'. As the apostle Paul makes clear to his good friend Timothy:

Everyone who wants to live a godly life in Christ Jesus will be persecuted.
2 Timothy 3:12

Now please be assured: no one is advocating masochism! We are not told to provoke rejection or actively to invite it. But we *are* told—and it is a subtle distinction—to expect it, as indeed many have before us.

How to combat fear

The fears of inadequacy, of losing our reputation and of rejection are very real fears. But we must not let them immobilize us. Romans 8:1 says, 'There is now no condemnation for those in Christ Jesus.'

Instead, we need to own up to these fears, and confess them. Let us be honest with ourselves and God, and make sure we are getting all the acceptance we need from him. What we need is to learn how to manage our fears, and subdue them. Then, like the disciples in Acts 4:29–31, we should learn to pray for boldness:

'Now, Lord, consider their threats and enable your servants to speak your word with great boldness. Stretch out your hand to heal and perform miraculous signs and wonders through the name of your holy servant Jesus.' After they prayed, the place where they were meeting was shaken. And they were all filled with the Holy Spirit and spoke the Word of God boldly.
Acts 4:29–31

Verification—a valuable tool

Is what you fear true? Honestly? You can find out! Later
in this chapter, the first exercise will provide you with
an extremely useful process. Its message is based on
the unwelcome fact that we often tell ourselves that our
fears *are* true. However, if we verify them, we discover
that many things we are afraid of are just plain lies! The
truth is often something different altogether.

Indeed, this process of verification may well be the
most important exercise you will come across in the
entire text. Learn to use it frequently. It is the starting
block for all the other exercises and it will help you
whenever you have a fear about anything. In evangelism,
as in everything else we do, we won't get anywhere—
except stuck—if it's fear that determines our actions.

Be positive

If, however, you aren't immobilized by fear, but you
are just plain pessimistic by nature, take a tip from the
tortoise: you won't make any progress if you don't
stick your neck out! Remember that if David had been
a pessimist, he would have looked at Goliath and said,
'Oh no, he's huge! He's a giant! I want to run away!'
But he didn't. Instead, he probably said, 'Great, he's
huge! How can I miss?!'

Exercise One

What are your fears as you consider speaking to your
friends? Imagine that I have just asked you to go to
your neighbour with the express intention of telling

them about Jesus. Use your notebook to put down all your thoughts.

1. First, write down the demand: *Go to my neighbour and tell them about Jesus.*

2. Second, listen for the fear. Write down: *My mind tells me...* **and shut your eyes briefly, listening to everything you can hear your mind saying.**

3. Thirdly, name those fears! Write them down—go on, every one, however silly they may look on paper!

4. Verify them, as follows: when you have finished your list of statements, write down against each one T (true), F (false) or D/K (don't know).

Remember that *any statement you hold to be true about the future is actually a 'don't know'—no one knows what will happen in the future until he or she tries it out.* **(When you don't know, it's not a truth, it's just a don't know. In fact, as a truth, it's false!)**

FOR EXAMPLE:

1. Demand: *Go to my neighbour and tell them about Jesus.*

2. My mind tells me:

They'll think I'm off my head...

If I fail, I'll be a useless Christian...

I'll be unlovable...

My friend has told me to go and evangelize and I respect her opinion...

They'll shut the door in my face...

There won't be anyone in...

They like me so I'm sure they'll want to hear all about it...

3. Verify:

They'll think I'm off my head... D/K (Have you asked them? You don't know what they'll think until you do.)

If I fail, I'll be a useless Christian... F (Useless in whose eyes?)

I'll be unlovable... F (Really?)

My friend has told me to go and evangelize and I respect her opinion... T

They'll shut the door in my face... D/K (Like the first one, how do you know this will happen?)

There won't be anyone in... D/K (Ditto!)

They like me so I'm sure they'll want to hear all about it... D/K (Ditto again!)

5. Spend some time confessing these fears and assumptions to the Lord.

6. Say out loud each statement, and whether it is true, false, or you don't know. Don't be shy. Only God is listening, and he knows the truth anyway. And you really need to get past these fears!

7. Finally, write out again and say out loud *only* the statements against which you have written 'True'; in

**this case, 'My friend has told me to go and
evangelize and I respect her opinion.'**

There are usually very few true statements, and often
there are none! In other words, we are actually far freer
to take action than our minds would have us believe!

For some people, these assumptions and fears may be
very deep-rooted, and you may find it helpful to seek a
friend who can pray with you for inner healing. But take
heart. It can also be quite liberating to do this exercise
just as it stands, with no extra help. To distinguish out
loud what is really true and what is not helps you to see
and feel clearly. The truth really will set you free!

Now pray for the Holy Spirit to come and heal you,
and give you boldness. Don't hurry this bit—it may be
that God wants to move deeply and powerfully within
you. If necessary, you can do the rest of this chapter's
work at another time.

Exercise Two

This exercise is designed to identify what we are being
asked to do. Write down two or three definitions of
the term evangelism. Reread any part of this chapter to
help you, but try to use your own words and say what
you really mean.

Exercise Three

Our church leaders have urged us to engage in a
decade of evangelism. Is that why you should

participate? What reasons can you give as to why you should evangelize? Write these down.

At a later date, if you wish, you can discuss them with family and friends and members of your church.

Daily Studies

The following readings are for your personal use during the week prior to the next chapter. Try and give a little time every day to each reading. Also, go back over the text of this chapter and your own notes. Be clear about the truth of any fears you may have. Spend time thinking about the list of reasons for evangelism (both mine and yours) and familiarize yourself with them.

Day one

Read Luke 15:3–7.

This passage shows the priority of evangelism. The shepherd is willing to risk leaving the ninety-nine sheep to reach the lost one. We cannot just hope that the lost one will come back to the fold, we must go out from the fold and find the lost one (Luke 15:8–32). From the parable of the Lost Sheep to the parables of the Lost Coin and the Lost Son, it's as though Jesus is trying to reinforce his point. Every lost person matters to God. Pause and reflect on the parable of the Lost Sheep.

Prayer

Do you know people who used to be Christians but are no longer committed? Pray for them. Ask the Lord to show you if you should do anything.

> *Lord, look through my eyes,*
> *Listen through my ears,*
> *Speak through my lips,*
> *Act with my hands,*
> *Walk with my feet. Amen.*

Day two

Read Mark 4:30–32.

Jesus predicted the growth of his kingdom from a small beginning. It is good to notice how this prediction has been proven true over the past 2,000 years. Look back at the growth of the church in the book of Acts, and be encouraged that it continues to grow.

Spend a few moments praising and thanking the Lord that his word is bearing fruit, and then praying for the continued growth of the church.

Prayer

> *O Lord Christ, who called your disciples not only to follow you but to become fishers of humankind, give to us and to your whole church grace to obey your word. Grant that, attempting great things for you, we may also*

*expect great things from you; to whom be
glory for ever and ever. Amen.*

Day three

Read Matthew 9:35–38.

Notice the word 'harassed' in verse 36; this word in
the Greek means 'whipped and beaten'. There are
many today burdened with fears, anxieties and guilt.

Now notice the word 'compassion' in the same
verse. In his book *A Call to Conversion*, Jim Wallis
writes:

*A very wise old man once told me the difference
between concern and compassion. Being
concerned is seeing something awful happening
and feeling, hey, that's really too bad. Having
compassion, he said, is seeing the same thing and
saying, 'I just can't let that happen', and
obviously trying to do something about it.*

Reflection

No one person can change the world. But we can
change the world for one person.

Prayer

Ask God to lay on your heart people and situations for
which you can intercede:

Lord, teach me to pray, to want to pray, to delight to pray. When I pray, teach me to pray with faith, with hope, with love. Let me make prayer my first work, my persistent work, my most important work. Let my prayer be a channel for your love, your peace, for those for whom I pray, and for myself. O dear and blessed Lord, Amen.

Eric Milner White

Day four

Read again Matthew 9:35–38.

Reflect on Jesus' comment in verse 37 and his encouragement to pray for more labourers in verse 38. In your notebook, make a list of all those you know— you may have personal contact with them or you may not—who are employed in missionary work.

Reflection

Pray for us; pray that the Lord's message may spread quickly, and be received with honour as it was among you; and pray that we may be preserved from the interference of bigoted, evil people.

2 Thessalonians 3:1 (Jerusalem Bible)

Pray for those listed and then pray for more labourers to go out into the harvest field. Pray for some people from your church to be called.

Day five

Read 1 Corinthians 12:12–31.

The most used term in the Bible for the church is 'the body of Christ'. The church is a body, not a business; that means the church is alive. All living things grow.

Spend some time praying for the leaders and staff of your church. Write down their names and pray for God's grace, wisdom and protection to be given to them.

Prayer

Pray for the growth of the church.

> *Simeon took the baby Jesus in his arms and praised God saying:*
> *Sovereign Lord, as you have promised,*
> *you now dismiss your servant in peace.*
> *For my eyes have seen your salvation,*
> *which you have prepared in the sight of all people.*
> **Luke 2: 29–31**

Read again 1 Corinthians 12:12–31. Remember that although none of us measures up to Christ as individuals, together we may do so. Each person has a part to play. Spend some time praying about what your part is in furthering God's kingdom.

In your notebook, write down what you are currently doing for God. Write down also what else you sense the Spirit of God is guiding you to do.

Spend some time praying about what you have written. Ask the Lord for confirmation and wisdom to know the next step.

> *Christ has no body now on earth but yours,*
> *no hands but yours, no feet but yours. Yours*
> *are the eyes through which you must look*
> *out with Christ's compassion on the world.*
> *Yours are the feet with which he is to go*
> *about doing good. Yours are the hands with*
> *which he blesses now. Amen.*
>
> **Teresa of Avila**

Day six

Read 1 Corinthians 9:19–23. Notice in particular this verse:

> *So that by all possible means I might save some.*
>
> **1 Corinthians 9:22**

Courses and books on evangelism are only useful if they help us to be effective witnesses to the good news. If all they do is pass on interesting information or fuel discussions, then the courses have failed.

Prayer

Spend some time praying for this course. Pray for yourself. Pray for the Spirit's illumination to help you to think through your progress. Pray for wisdom to know what needs to be applied personally and what needs to be done corporately, by the body of the church. Pray for God's Holy Spirit to inspire us with the same urgency and passion that the apostle Paul had in today's reading.

> *Take, Lord, all my liberty, my memory, my understanding and my whole will. You have given me all that I have, all that I am, and I surrender all to your divine will, that you dispose of me. Give me only your love and your grace. With this I am rich enough, and have no more to ask. Amen.*

Ignatius of Loyola

CHAPTER 2

What is the good news that we share?

To be an effective witness we must get the story out, but get the story straight! *It is obvious that many people's understanding of Christianity is a misunderstanding.* It is therefore vital for Christians to know what they believe and why they believe it.

I sometimes tell the following joke, because it so clearly represents people's misunderstandings. It's about a priest who goes into a bar and tells everyone that heaven is not only a great place but that he can also tell them how to get there. Who, he asks, would like to go? Lots of people smile and put their hands up in the general cheeriness of the surroundings, except for one man who is clearly quite happy just sitting in his corner with his drink.

The priest is concerned. 'Come now,' he says, 'do you really not want to go to heaven after you die?'

'Oh,' replies the man, surprised, '... after I *die*; I thought you were taking a party *now*.'

The wrong signals

So often the signals we send out are confusing ones. Sometimes, we send clear messages—for example, when the Roman Catholic conclaves choose a new

Pope. The custom is that the secret ballots of the cardinals are burned after each vote and black smoke comes billowing out; but when a new Pope has been elected a chemical is added so that white smoke comes out, to indicate that the decision has been made.

But did you know that at one election not enough chemical was added and the smoke came out grey! The wondering crowd outside were left in confusion—did they, or did they not, have a new pope? Had he just had a heart attack? Was he only a 'sort of pope'... not really a proper one?!

For some people, this incident might seem rather trivial and even funny, but it did cause genuine consternation at the time. At a deeper level, all Christians everywhere do need to consider this question: can they afford to pass on muddled messages? I don't think so. They simply cannot risk confusion if they are to make the impact on our generation that God expects of us.

> For 'if the trumpet does not sound with a clear call, who will get ready for battle?'
> **1 Corinthians 14:8**

Misconceptions about Christianity

Some of my friends are not at all religious. They freely admit it, and in no way do I condemn them for their views. In fact, I feel very deeply for them. Organized religion totally turns them off, so they see no need to investigate the subject. This being turned off, however, may be because they judge Jesus Christ by what they can see on the surface of 'the church'. Perhaps they are rejecting the king because they don't like the look of the subjects.

Then there's a second group of people I know, who say they are religious but who have a seriously inaccurate picture of what a Christian really is. I feel for them, too. They're the sort of people who watch religious TV programmes and are always ready to discuss religion. Yet all the time they have a sense of incompleteness about their faith.

They're what might be called the hatch-match-dispatch group; they go to church when they're christened, they go when they marry and they go after they die. What's more, on only one of these occasions do they go out of choice—the other times they have to be carried in!

Here are some misconceptions about what a Christian is from some interviewees in Nottingham:

I'm Church of England.

I'm a very nice person.

I got married in a church thirty-four years ago.

Well, I had a great-aunt who played the organ in church...

Misconceptions about God

Imagine you have a six-year-old daughter, and she comes to you and says, 'Mummy, is God everywhere?'

You are happy to have this conversation. It is a comfortable one for you both. 'Yes!' you say, confidently. 'God is everywhere.'

But your daughter is a little scientist. She wants to find out how this idea really works. 'Mummy, if God is everywhere, is he in our kitchen?'

'Yes!' you say, confidently, again.

Your daughter persists. 'Mummy, if God is in our kitchen, is he in this cupboard?'

'Yes!' you say, still confidently, but beginning to wonder what is coming next.

'Mummy, if God is in this cupboard, is he in our marmalade jar?'

Your daughter is holding out the marmalade jar for you to see.

You agree, although definitely puzzled now, that God is certainly in your marmalade jar.

'Good!' says your daughter, as she slams the lid on. 'Got him!'

Unfortunately, all we get is a bad start if we try to assess God as we would anyone else. We cannot 'psych' him out. If you and I could understand God he wouldn't be worth believing in. He is greater than all of our minds put together.

God is a mystery to be enjoyed, not a problem to be solved. Rather than a riddle which alienates us, God should be a mystery that fascinates and beckons.

This is the sense of wonder that one of the writers of the New Testament captures:

Oh, the depth of the riches of the wisdom and knowledge of God! How unsearchable his judgments, and his paths beyond tracing out! To him be the glory for ever.

Romans 11:33–36

God cannot be boxed into the narrow confines of our expectations. God is different and delightfully so! The God of the Bible confirmed by many Christians is truth wrapped in surprise and wonder. Words cannot be found to explain him and yet he relates to us personally, at the very centre of our being.

Misconceptions about knowledge

One of the problems we all experience in trying to fathom out both Christianity and God is that there are different kinds of knowledge. Often, one kind has no bearing on a question belonging to another kind.

The first kind of knowledge is logic; this includes linear thinking, and rational, calculative and mathematical findings. When we learn how to add two and two, we will come to know and understand the existence of four.

When physicists planned the journey of the Hubbell telescope, they needed not to love outer space, but to calculate how to get there.

Secondly, there's scientific knowledge: you have a hypothesis, and you test it. This kind of knowledge includes supposition, the trial of that supposition in a controlled environment, consequent evidence and what can, on that basis, be called proof. A new drug may save lives, but cause blindness. Every step in all the hypotheses in the drug's development must be tested before it is either used or discarded.

But there is also a third kind of knowledge: personal knowledge—if you like, the knowledge of the heart, or spirit.

For example, if I would like to kiss my wife, I don't say to myself, 'Ah, I know what's coming next. It's the addition of two lips to two more lips with a bit of suction thrown in, along with the exchange of microbes and carbon dioxide.'

Nor do I hypothesize about the specific measure of pressure needed on the component parts, in order to produce a measurable response!

What I do know is simply that I love—and love enough to give a tender and heartfelt sign of that love to another human being.

Christianity, God, and our admittedly limited knowledge about both, all belong to the personal realm. They are not so much deduced, or quantitatively measured; rather they are *experienced*; they are lived.

The good news diagram

During this chapter you will learn to explain the good news clearly, through a diagram which can be used whenever the opportunity arises. The diagram is based on the stories in the early chapters of Genesis.

The one thing you *shouldn't* be doing as you learn this is to spend time worrying about whether or not Adam and Eve actually existed, or whether the human race began instantly or evolved over time. The issue is not about how we got here, it's about what happens now we are. The important thing for this chapter is to learn about the *underlying truths* expressed in these chapters at the very beginning of the Bible.

God

In the beginning, before there was anything else, there was God.

GOD

Then, God made the world.

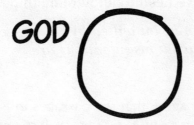

In the beginning God created the heavens and the earth. Now the earth was formless and empty, darkness was over the surface of the deep and the Spirit of God was hovering over the waters.

Genesis 1:1–2

See Genesis 1 for how he made the world.

Evil enters the world

We now introduce Satan into the picture. It has been said that some Christians either know nothing about

GOD ◯ SATAN

him or have an unhealthy interest in him. It is important that we do not hold either of these positions. But we need to know something:

> *So we will not be outwitted by Satan—we know well enough what his intentions are.*
> **2 Corinthians 2:11**

Most expositors agree that the passages in Isaiah 14 and Ezekiel 28 look beyond the Kings of Tyre and Babylon and are detailed descriptions of the person of Satan.

Originally, of course, Satan was created by God (Colossians 1:16). Made like his creator, completely free to exercise his will, Satan could do or not do the will of God as he saw fit. He had the power to revolt if he wanted to. It was not suspected that he would covet his maker's throne, for he seemingly held every honour but that. However, with his free will Satan chose to rebel, and Genesis 3 gives the story of his influence over the world.

> *Your behaviour was exemplary from the day of your creation until the day when evil was first found in you... And so I threw you to the earth.*
> **Ezekiel 28:15**

Jesus refers to Satan as 'the prince of this world' (John 14:30). The apostle Paul refers to Satan as 'the god of this age' (2 Corinthians 4:4). The apostle John says: 'The world is under the control of the evil one' (1 John 5:19).

The tree of life

In the garden of Eden, God planted two trees, the first of which was the tree of life. This represents all the good things of God.

> *And the Lord God made all kinds of trees grow...*
> *In the middle of the garden were the tree of life*
> *and the tree of the knowledge of good and evil.*
> **Genesis 2:9**

The tree of knowledge of good and evil

The other tree in the garden was the tree of knowledge of good and evil. This represents the choice we have to make: either good or evil. To choose evil means death.

Man and woman

Man and woman are created to enjoy the gift of life, but with the ability to choose either good or evil (Genesis 1:26–28).

Now the Lord God had planted a garden in the east, in Eden, and there he put the man he had formed.

And the Lord God commanded the man, 'You are free to eat from any tree in the garden, but you must not eat from the tree of knowledge of good and evil, for when you eat of it you will surely die.'

Genesis 2:8, 16–17

Satan's influence

Now the Serpent [Satan] was more crafty...,
encouraging Adam and Eve to eat of the tree of
the knowledge of good and evil. And so Eve
*'... took some and ate it. She also gave some to
her husband who was with her and he ate it.'*
(Genesis 3:1, 6)

In other words, Satan tempted them to disobey God and, like Satan, they rebelled. As a result they were cut off from God and the tree of life (Genesis 3:21–24).

Since then, people have endeavoured to reach God, but no amount of *self*-effort has made this possible. So we became, and still become, stuck. What on earth can the human race do? What can happen next, if anything?

Just for a moment, imagine that you and everyone you know are trapped in a room with me. I will never let any of you leave. You can't escape, because I am stronger than all of you put together and I have locked all the exits. You are trapped. No matter what you try to do, you just can't get out. Is there an answer?

Well, you *could* escape if someone outside the room, who is stronger than I am, broke down the door and rescued you.

The cross of Jesus—God's rescue act

That's a bit like what God has done for us. If we were to sum it up in one word, we would use the word 'rescue'. God's action in the cross is a rescue act, reaching down to the deepest point of our need.

The word the Bible uses for 'rescue' is 'redeem'. The word for 'rescuer' is 'redeemer'. A redeemer is a great benefactor who frees slaves by actually paying a ransom price for them.

The great mediator

The cross is the movement of God towards the people he loves—both you and me. The cross unites separated parties. The Bible's word for this is 'reconciliation'. The cross of Jesus enabled God and humankind to meet on new terms so that now, through the one mediator, Jesus Christ, we can enter again into a direct relationship with God.

This is what Jesus Christ has done for people through the cross, because in him God is here: the invisible becomes visible; the intangible becomes tangible; and the unknowable becomes knowable—all in order to rescue *us*.

So now in Christ, we have redemption through his blood.

Ephesians 1:7

Accepting Christ

We therefore can come to God through Jesus.

◆ We admit that we have been deceived by Satan and have sinned.

◆ We commit our lives to God.

◆ We submit our lives to the teaching of Jesus.

◆ We transmit the message of Jesus to a world longing to hear the good news.

Two helpful metaphors

The key to natural evangelism is to be natural! Just be your normal self. We saw in Chapter 1 how Jesus used everyday stories about commonplace events and objects to reveal profound truths. Today, simple, everyday images and metaphors can still help to reveal truth in important ways.

The first metaphor is based on the concept of a bank account. If I owe you money and you owe me money, but we are both overdrawn at the bank, neither of us can cash a cheque and repay the other. Our accounts are no good. We both need a third person who is, as it were, in credit with the bank, in order for us to repay our debts both to each other and to the banker. Jesus is in the position of being the only one in credit. It is to him we can turn, in undeserving gratitude, to help us pay off our debts. What's more, he charges us nothing in return.

The second metaphor is based on a story about sacrifice. It concerns a kind person, a bus driver, whose job it was to collect all the children from a certain rural district and take them to and from school every day. One evening, when he was bringing the children home, he realized to his horror that the brakes had failed as the bus sped down the final hill home.

His only solution was somehow to break the progress of the bus. To his right the hillside fell away steeply. He knew that if he steered the bus over the edge, he could probably throw himself clear through the driver's side door—but he certainly couldn't save the children.

To his left and a little further on, however, he knew there was a field where he could roll the bus over to the left. It was a risk, and he couldn't throw himself clear in the same way, but there was a good chance that everyone would survive.

So the bus careered on down the hill, and the driver skillfully prepared to turn the bus into the field. Tragically, there was a young child playing at the gate. The driver had run out of time. He had to decide. He saw the child clearly. But he turned the bus over.

Soon afterwards, all the families had gathered around, overcome with gratitude that their children were safe. One by one everyone went home, bruised and shaky, but glad to be alive. Everyone, that is, except for one grandmother who went to thank the bus driver for his skill and courage.

But the driver was in a state of shock. The child so tragically killed at the gate of the field had been his own son.

There is, of course, one important difference between this son, and Jesus the Son of God. In a way, it makes the point even sharper. The little boy at the gate didn't have a choice. Jesus did.

These are just two ways of explaining the Christian message. Try to know several different ways of explaining it. Read evangelistic booklets like *Journey into Life* by Norman Warren and *Game of Life* by J. John! And more substantial books like *Questions of Life* by Nicky Gumbel and *Dead Sure* by J. John!

Being a Christian

Those who are captured by Jesus Christ want to captivate others for Jesus. Remember that, ultimately, being a Christian involves four main elements, however you interpret the detail of them:

◆ **Accept:** take to heart the truth underlying the life, death and resurrection of Jesus Christ.

◆ **Commit:** commit yourself to Jesus so that God can live in you.

◆ **Submit:** be obedient to *his* teaching and *his* will, so that you mature in the love of God.

◆ **Transmit:** pass on this love to others.

Exercise One

Ask yourself, 'What is a Christian?' Explain it to yourself as if it were new to you. Try not to use words like 'salvation' or 'Pentecost'. Remember, you are not trying to attempt a long explanation, but just a few words in a couple of sentences. Write it down in your notebook.
Once you have written it down, think hard.

◆ Would this explanation be helpful to an unbeliever?

◆ Did you use jargon?—be honest!!

Exercise Two

For this exercise, you need to have learnt the good news diagram, so that you can be very familiar with it and use it easily. For some people this kind of thing brings back all sorts of schoolday fears of failure—but really, this is not an exam! Understand each part of it thoroughly and don't be afraid to take your time over it. We are all learning.
See if you can use the diagram to explain the good news. Then try the whole exercise afresh without looking at the diagram you have already drawn; instead, try drawing a new one from memory. (But if you need to have a look then do so.) Don't take too

long over it and, please, the main idea is just to get a feel of it, so that you can begin to learn how to use it. Practise redrawing the diagram for yourself.

Daily Studies

Is there anything new you have discovered about the good news? As part of your studies this week, familiarize yourself with the diagram. To get it into your head, draw it out at every opportunity! Better still, try it out on a friend who is not a Christian. They may have been wanting someone to explain the gospel to them for years.

Day one

I believe in God, the Father Almighty, Maker of heaven and earth.
The Apostles' Creed

Read Acts 17:16–29.

Jesus addressed God as *Abba*, an Aramaic word which means 'Daddy'. 'Abba, Father,' he said, 'everything is possible for you. Take this cup from me. Yet not what I will, but what you will' (Mark 14:36).

When Jesus called God 'Abba', he was expressing his own intimate relationship with God. Paul also uses the word in his letter to the Romans:

For you did not receive a Spirit that makes you a slave again to fear, but the Spirit makes you God's children. And by him we cry 'Abba, my Father!'

Romans 8:15

And in Galatians:

Because you are his children, God sent the Spirit of his Son into our hearts, the Spirit who calls out 'Abba, my Father!'

Galatians 4:6

Jesus was the first to apply the term 'Abba' to God, and he gave authority to his disciples to do so. The apostle Paul sees in its use a symbol of the Christian's adoption as a child of God and their possession of the Spirit.

Many people today have a bad father image because of their human parent model. Pray that we may afresh know, trust and experience God as our Father. And pray that he may bring his healing to those who have a marred perception of him.

Prayer

Father, I abandon myself into your hands; do with me what you will. Whatever you may do, I thank you; I am ready for all, I accept all. Let your will be done in me. I wish no more than this, O Lord. Into your hands I commend my soul; I offer it to you with all

*the love of my heart. For I love you, Lord,
and so wish to give myself, to surrender
myself into your hands without reserve and
with boundless confidence, for you are my
father. Amen.*

Day two

*I believe in Jesus Christ, his only Son, our Lord,
who was conceived by the Holy Spirit, born of the
virgin Mary.*

The Apostles' Creed

Read Matthew 1:18–2:12.

Messiah is a Hebrew word which means 'anointed
one'. In the Greek language it is translated to
Christos—Christ. The Nicene Creed continues and says
of Jesus that he is:

*God from God, light from light, true God from
true God, begotten, not made, one in being with
the Father.*

The Nicene Creed

All these words have been calculated to emphasize that
in Jesus it is the God of creation who meets us and saves
us. In Jesus we see and experience God. The Latin word
for Lord, *dominus*, means 'one who owns slaves'. In
other words, your Lord is someone who has ownership
over you. When we call Jesus 'Lord', we acknowledge
and profess that Jesus is the one who owns our loyalty.

This idea may seem unreal for us today. But in the early church, the worship of the Caesar was the official religion of the Roman Empire. Once every year all citizens of the Empire had to appear before the magistrates in order to burn a pinch of incense to the godhead of Caesar while saying 'Caesar is Lord'.

But Jesus Christ alone is Lord and many Christians, refusing to deny that fact, submitted to persecution, imprisonment and martyrdom.

If he is not Lord of all, he is not Lord at all.
Anonymous

Prayer

Pray that we will not only know God as Father, but also as Lord. Pray that we will have a sense of awe, respect and humility. Pray that Jesus may be Lord of all in the church and that inconsistencies in our own life and church may be put right.

Lord Jesus Christ, Son of God,
have mercy on me, a sinner.
The Jesus Prayer of the Orthodox Church

Day three

He suffered under Pontius Pilate, was crucified,
dead and buried. He descended to the dead.
The Apostles' Creed

Read John 18:28–19:22.

The word atonement means 'the bringing together of two estranged and separated parties'. Sin originated when, through our own free will, we turned our back on God.

We were created in God's likeness to live in the world and to enjoy an intimate relationship with him. Because God is love, we were not forced into this relationship; we were given the free will to choose, to accept or to reject God. But we have turned away from God. This has had the immediate effect, whenever it has happened, of cutting us off from him.

The basic meaning of the life, death and resurrection of Jesus is that:

> *God was reconciling the world to himself in Christ.*
>
> **2 Corinthians 5:19**

> *Jesus died so that we, living or dying, might be truly at one with God because of Christ's forgiveness, so that nothing in all creation, not even death itself, will ever again separate us from God's presence.*
>
> **Romans 8:31–39**

> *If Jesus Christ were to come today, people would not crucify him. They would ask him to dinner and hear what he had to say and then make fun of him.*
>
> **Thomas Carlyle**

Prayer

Let us reflect and thank Jesus for all the suffering he went through to enable us to be part of the family of God. This is the key that many people need to find truth and life.

> *Teach us, good Lord, to serve you as you deserve,*
> *to give and not to count the cost,*
> *to fight and not to heed the wounds,*
> *to toil and not to seek for rest,*
> *to labour and not to ask for any reward*
> *save that of knowing that we do your will.*
> *Amen.*
>
> **Ignatius of Loyola**

Day four

> *The third day he rose again from the dead.*
>
> **The Apostles' Creed**

Read John 20:1–29.

In many churches on Easter Sunday, the minister will say, 'Christ is risen,' and the congregation respond, 'He is risen indeed.'

> *The resurrection of Jesus Christ from the dead is the foundation of Christianity: if he did not rise from the dead, then there is no truth in Christianity—it does not have anything to stand on. Christianity as a religion is unique because it*

is based on the death and resurrection of its founder. So either it is the biggest hoax in the history of the world or it is true.

Without the resurrection, the Christian movement would have petered out in ignominy and there would have been no Christianity. It is not too much to say that without the resurrection, the phenomenon of Christianity in the apostolic age—and since—is scientifically unaccountable. It is also true to say that without the resurrection Christianity would not be itself, as the distinctiveness of Christianity is not its adherence to a teacher who lived long ago, but in its belief that 'Jesus is Lord' for every generation through the centuries.

Michael Ramsey, former Archbishop of Canterbury

Prayer

Were not our hearts burning within us while he talked with us on the road and opened the scriptures to us?

Luke 24:32

Let us pray that we will know the resurrected Jesus in a new way today. Pray that our experience of him may be similar to that of the two disciples whom he met on the road to Emmaus.

You are the light of minds that know you; the life of souls that love you; and the strength of wills that serve you. Help us to know you so that we may truly love you; help us to love

you so that we may fully serve you, because
in serving you we find perfect freedom.
Amen.

Augustine of Hippo

Day five

He ascended into heaven and is seated at the
right hand of the Father.

The Apostles' Creed

Read Acts 1:6–11.

The word ascension is used to describe the departure
of Jesus from the earth. Ascension Day is celebrated
forty days after Easter (Acts 1:3). Jesus Christ returned
to his Father and so to the place of power and
authority. The ascension shows that Jesus:

◆ has completed his redeeming work on earth
(Hebrews 9:24–26);

◆ has gone ahead to prepare a place for his followers
(John 14:2);

◆ prays for us (Hebrews 7:25; Romans 8:34);

◆ rules with his Father (Hebrews 1:3);

◆ is waiting to return to establish the kingdom of God
(1 Corinthians 15:24).

What wonderful truths and thoughts these are for us
while we wait and persevere in his service. Pray today
that these truths will inspire us to 'good works'.

Prayer

*Lord, grant me the grace of a deep, fervent
and living faith in you and all that you have
revealed. Take away all pride, vanity,
insincerity, self-interest, and anything that
may hinder me from accepting your truth.
Help me to trust in you and have strength and
wholeness. Lead me and guide me so that I
may grow in your love and holiness. Amen.*

Day six

*He will come to judge the living and the dead
and his kingdom will have no end.*
The Apostles' Creed

Read 2 Peter 3:1–13.

Three devils were talking and trying to decide how
they could keep Christians from being effective.

One devil said, 'I know, let's tell Christians that there
is no heaven. No possibility of rewards. That will keep
them quiet.'

Another devil said, 'No, let's just tell them there is
no hell. No possibility of punishment. That will keep
them quiet.'

And the third devil said, 'No, wait a minute. I've got
it! Let's not tell them there's no heaven or that there's
no hell. Let's just tell them there's plenty of time,
there's no hurry.'

There is so little time and so much to do. So let us labour in the vineyard.

Once a man is united to God, how could he not live forever? Once a man is separated from God, what can he do but wither and die?

C. S. Lewis

So we must:

◆ watch (Matthew 24:42);

◆ be ready (Matthew 24:44);

◆ guard our own spiritual lives (1 Corinthians 9:24–25);

◆ live faithfully (1 Peter 4:10);

◆ pray and work to 'seek and save the lost'—what this course is all about (Luke 19:10; John 20:21).

Prayer

Bestow on me, O Lord my God, an understanding that knows you, wisdom in finding you, a way of life that is pleasing to you, perseverance that faithfully waits for you and confidence that I may meet you at the end. Amen.

Thomas Aquinas

CHAPTER 3

What is natural evangelism?

I wonder how you first heard about Jesus? Was it your mum or dad telling you Bible stories, longer ago than you can remember? Was it a teacher at school for whom you had a special respect? Was it a friend?

I'll tell you where it wasn't—it wasn't at a big evangelistic meeting where people are called to commit themselves to the Lord! Many people do commit themselves at these meetings, but that's not how they first hear about it. They first hear about it from *someone they know*.

When I was a teenager, I first heard about Jesus properly from a friend of mine called Andy. After it had sunk in, I got so excited I told another friend of mine, Richard. Evangelism starts in normal, ordinary, everyday conversations. You're just having a natter and then someone says something that seems to switch a light on inside you, and you think, hey, what does that mean? And then you really start talking. It's just one friend talking to another.

Jerusalem, Judea and beyond

The evangelistic strategy given to us by Jesus is recorded in the opening chapter of Acts where Jesus said:

*You will receive power when the Holy Spirit
comes on you; and you will be my witnesses in
Jerusalem and in all Judea and Samaria and to
the ends of the earth.*
Acts 1:8

What we understand by the word 'power' can be both
good and bad, of course, but here the word actually
means *energy*. Do you ever feel your get up and go has
got up and gone? I do, frequently! But Jesus promises
us that the Holy Spirit will give real energy, and it is
one of the greatest assurances we have: that despite
our tiredness and staleness at times, the Holy Spirit
refreshes and empowers us in a remarkable way.

'Witnesses' are to be just that, people who tell what
they have seen and experienced to others who have
not yet heard about it. (Unfortunately, in the church
today, we are inclined to spend more time with
believers than with unbelievers. But it's really very
hard to catch fish in a pond where there aren't any!)

Then comes a bombshell: 'Jerusalem... Judea...
Samaria... and to the ends of the earth'. Jesus is not
talking about the disciples witnessing over some more
cosy suppers with another dozen or so friends on the
shores of Lake Galilee. They are to witness first, in
Jerusalem—the city; secondly, in Judea—the county;
thirdly, in Samaria—the next county; and fourthly,
throughout the ends of the earth (see diagram on next
page)!

Why does Jesus instruct his disciples to start in
Jerusalem? Because it was where they were, it was
their home. We, too, should start sharing where we
are. Our Jerusalem is our home—the immediate circle

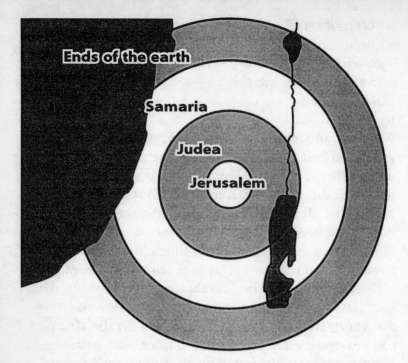

of our family and friends, neighbours, colleagues and so on.

The instruction is also a shock to the system for another reason. What was the disciples' track record like in Jerusalem? When Jesus was taken into custody, what happened to the disciples? All the disciples *deserted* him and ran away... and then Peter denied Jesus three times (Matthew 26:56, 69–75). *Jesus explicitly instructs them to start in their place of greatest failure*; and the uncomfortable but essential fact for us to grasp is that we have to start sharing in the place where we have been least effective as a witness.

Starting in Jerusalem

As we have seen, Jerusalem was not just 'home'; it was also the place of the disciples' failure. God might well call us to share our faith with those amongst whom we feel we have failed.

Who are the people with whom you may have failed to share Christ, in your close family and friends? If it seems such a tall order to begin here, start first by loving these people through prayer. Pray about your love for them, and the things you do and the things you say.

The next key stage to witnessing in places where we think we have failed is *to apologize*. Say, 'I'm sorry— I'm sorry I have never shared with you the thing that is most important to me.'

Then the gospel needs to move on. In the Acts of the Apostles, the gospel went 'from house to house' (Acts 20:20). So the gospel goes from your home to the homes of others you already know. There are three natural access areas:

◆ **Kinship**—those with whom we share a common kinship, our family and close friends.

◆ **Community**—the people we meet regularly: for example, the bus-driver, the window-cleaner, the newsagent, our neighbours.

◆ **Common interest**—those with whom we share the same meeting place, at a sports club, for instance, or an evening class, and so on.

Jesus' instruction to one new believer was:

> *Go home to your family and tell them how much*
> *the Lord has done for you.*
> **Mark 5:19**

Some of you might be thinking, 'If I go to my family and friends and tell them I'm a Christian, I'm going to feel awkward and embarrassed. They know what I am like!'

But Jesus constantly taught that if we are his followers, our lives will bear the stamp of profound love to God, to ourselves and to our neighbours.

Our sociology ought to reflect our theology. How we treat others will be the clearest signal of what we think God is like. The first Bible most people read will be our lives, long before they ever read the book. You and I are a witness whether we want to be one or not. Either we are a good one or a poor one. We may bring good news—or bad news. You and I may be the only Bible some people ever read.

The best way is just to be yourself. You could go to the person or people in question, or write or phone, saying, 'Could I just talk to you about something? It's only really just occurred to me that we have known each other for a long time now and I know you know that I am religious, but I have never really ever told you about the most important thing in my life. Would you forgive me? I've always considered you to be so close to me and it seems so silly, if that's true, that I haven't really explained it to you. Besides, how can I really value you and not share the most important thing in my life?'

What will the person's reaction be? Certainly forgiving, and by actually asking someone to forgive you in the first place you automatically show that something must have happened in your life. What's most important is that you are saying *I value you*.

So when you think about your 'Jerusalem', think whether you can care about someone and *not* share the most important thing in your life. Remember you are not going to preach at them, far from it. You are not going to give them a sermon, but share instead a few seeds of the grace of God you know about in your life.

Judea

We particularly concentrate on 'Jerusalem' in this course, because this is where natural evangelism begins to take place. However, once you are effective in evangelism in your own Jerusalem, you can start moving out.

Judea was further afield for the disciples, and it's the same for us. Judea represents the evangelism of those friends and contacts we don't see so regularly: our wider family perhaps, and those whom we would call acquaintances or distant colleagues rather than close friends. The process, however, is the same.

Samaria

Samaria, where the Samaritans lived, represented the enemies of the Jews. So the next place for you to evangelize is with people you do not necessarily like to begin with! In addition, they may not like you either, but at least you have a relationship with them, even if it is a bad one!

> *Love your enemies, do good to those who hate you.*
> **Luke:12–14**

Someone once said, '90 per cent of evangelism is love'. The apostle Paul wrote, 'Christ's love compels us because we are convinced that one died for all' (2 Corinthians 5:14); and the apostle John says, 'We love because he first loved us' (1 John 4:19).

If we love God we will love people—any people. And we cannot love other people without caring for them.

Jesus himself was labelled 'a friend of sinners' (Matthew 11:19), and one of the many things that are so intriguing about Jesus was that he was so comfortable with 'sinners' and they were so comfortable with him. A good question to ask is: 'Just how many Christians today do unbelievers care to be around?' A dozen? Three? Any at all?

However, we must remember that Jesus didn't spend all his time having a social chit-chat with 'sinners'; he also taught them about the kingdom of God. The 'danger' with our family, friends, colleagues, neighbours, acquaintances and, yes, even enemies, is that some of us are so keen on maintaining the relationships that we ignore the evangelism.

There is no relationship on earth that takes priority over our loyalty to Jesus Christ and we must remember his example above all others: Jesus lovingly pointed out to Nicodemus, an older man with considerable prestige, that he was ignorant of heavenly things (John 3); Jesus also lovingly told the Samaritan woman that she could never worship God without facing up to her moral sin (John 4).

In other words, *the relationships that Christ formed—close and distant—led directly to confrontation*. And he kept loving people even when they rejected him (The Rich Ruler—Mark 10:21).

The ends of the earth

It is only after we have begun in a natural way, speaking to those we are very close to, followed by those with whom we are merely acquainted, followed by those whom initially we may actively dislike, that we are ready to move on. Then, and only then, are we ready to witness 'to the ends of the earth'. This phrase represents the evangelism of those we do not know, through missions, door to door visiting, and so forth.

So when we share the gospel we start with the people closest to us and we move out in ever-growing circles.

Why do people come to church?

We have looked at what Jesus told his disciples to do and where they were to do it. Let's now look at some statistics about what attracts people into coming to church:

◆ One per cent come because they have been visited by church members. This figure can vary enormously from area to area. In some places where I have conducted missions, pastoral visiting has produced much fruit. In other areas, however, this figure is miserably low.

71

◆ Two per cent come because of the church programme—for example, a ministry for the deaf, a children's holiday club, meetings for senior citizens, the provision of lunches, and so on.

◆ Three per cent come out of a special need—often because of a bereavement.

◆ Four per cent come because of Sunday school.

◆ Six per cent walk through the door because they see some publicity.

◆ Eight per cent come because of personal contact with the ministers and other church staff, perhaps through hospital visiting, marriage preparation, or counselling.

◆ Seventy-seven per cent come because they were invited by friends and relatives.

It's worth taking a moment just to think about that.

Where is your Jerusalem? With whom do you share a common kinship, community and interest? Who would you like to come with you to church? You need to identify these before you do anything further. In the first exercise at the end of this chapter, you will be invited to write down the names you come up with. For now, though, just focus on some of these names and have them in mind as you move on to the next section.

Sowing the seed

It is often overlooked, but no farmer on earth, nor Jesus, ever suggested we should put fully-grown plants into the ground in order to harvest their produce! This is not so much because it would be economically stupid, as because the fully-grown plant simply will not take to the ordinary soil. We are only asked to sow *seeds* to begin with: a word, a kindly action, an ear that is truly sensitive to the felt need of someone in trouble.

Of course, it is important that we sow generously, but it is still tiny seeds that we need to sow. Our tendency, unfortunately, is to focus on one person and be 'over-generous' (to put it kindly). We try and sow a plant!

Then we focus on that one plant, and we drown it in water, we watch it like a hawk, we fertilize it like crazy with one Bible verse and one 'holy experience' after another! Even though there is much more garden growing up around us, we are focused on the one plant, one person—and how!

This was not Jesus' advice. Sometimes, when I have sown the seed in someone I really like, I want them to become a Christian *urgently* and I get preoccupied with them (like a pregnancy!). But it may not be time for the birth; and there are others who are ready to help with that when the time is right.

Our job is to sow—and to sow only seeds, that are tiny. It is God who will produce the crop. Later in the process, of course, we must be around so that God can say to us, 'It's time to harvest, or sow again, or fertilize a little or cultivate or water.' But we can't make the seeds grow or mature or ripen the fruit. We are sowers and harvesters, and if we learn to do those things well we won't get frustrated trying to make the fruit mature.

Some of the best and most natural evangelism we can do might be to sow the seeds of kindness or concern of love that we show someone over a period of time. I once came across an extremely keen Christian couple who were very lively members of a very lively church. But when they were asked how they evangelized, the husband looked embarrassed. He explained that he and his wife were not great speakers, but that they tried to work for God in two ways: his wife took in babies and children abandoned by their parents; and he himself helped at an old people's home, to help people have their baths. He had no need to be embarrassed. These are wonderful examples of true seed-sowing, not plant-throwing!

To do such things is also to share the fruits of the Spirit, and if we do this generously then 'God is able to make all grace abound' (2 Corinthians 9:8). The promise is that as we share and sow our time, energy and resources with those who do not know God, then his grace will be all around us.

When the seeds begin to grow

When the seeds begin to grow—it may be you who have sown it or it may have been someone else— people will begin to drop some tell-tale remarks that they are interested in more. Have a listening ear to where they are at, to what they are really trying to say. They might say, 'I remember when I used to go to Sunday school'; or 'I was married in church'; or 'Well, I did get confirmed'; or even, 'Things have been difficult since my mum died.'

Remember, too, that God has appointed us 'Christian information officers'—we can also *expect* people to be interested. Don't be afraid to ask what someone believes and what involvement they have already had in the Christian faith. What do they think of it? Can you invite them to a *suitable* meeting or service.

Also, be positive! We often say, in a voice which has admitted defeat before we have even got an answer, 'I don't suppose you would be free on Sunday evening to come to a special service at our church?' Or: 'I know it's not really your scene, but you might find it interesting.'

Instead, prayerfully expect people to be intrigued and interested! I remember once an Asian girl, who became a Christian through a very timid and shy Christian. At her baptism, in her testimony, the Asian girl said, 'My Christian friend built a bridge from her heart to mine and Christ walked over it.'

In a nutshell

I repeat what I told you once before when we feared we might be left without a radio station: God's best microphone is Christ and Christ's best microphone is the church, and the church is all of us. Let each one of us, in our own job, in our own vocations—mum, married and single people, bishop, priest, deacon, high school or college student, workman, labourer—each one in our own place live in the faith intensely and feel that in our surroundings we are a true microphone of God our Lord.

Oscar Romeo

Let us start in 'our Jerusalem', our part of the world.

◆ Start loving people through prayer.

◆ Where you think you may have failed, apologize.

◆ Sow the seed of the gospel generously, but sensitively, on an 'as need' basis.

◆ Expect people to be interested, but have a listening ear to where *they* are at.

◆ Ask them what they believe—don't be afraid to do this.

◆ Make use of Christian tapes and books.

◆ Invite them to a suitable meeting or service.

Exercise One

In the New Testament, the good news was often spread through existing relationships. Look up the following passages, and then in your notebooks write out the following sentences and fill in the blanks (you can find the answers at the end of this chapter if you need them).

1. Andrew brought _____ (John 1:41)

2. Philip told _____ (John 1:43–45) (Notice that Philip, Andrew and Peter were all from the same area)

3. The Samaritan woman told _____ (John 4:28–30)

4. Levi invited _____
(Luke 5:27–32)

5. The Philippian jailer shared with _____
(Acts 16:25–34)

6. Day after day, in the temple courts and
_____ **they never stopped teaching and**
proclaiming the good news that Jesus is the Christ.
(Acts 5:42)

7. You know that I have not hesitated to preach
anything that would be helpful to you, but have
taught you publicly and _____
(Acts 20:20)

After you have done this, think about what you have
discovered about friendship from this exercise. Write
down any thoughts you have.

Exercise Two

This exercise is very important, so make sure you can
give plenty of time to it.

Take a few minutes now to write down in your
notebook the names of some people you know
personally who are not Christians (yet!) and with whom
it would be possible for you to share the good news
(see diagram on page 78).

Now, offer to God the names of these people whom
he created and loves. Pray that in the weeks and
months ahead the Spirit will give you the energy and
the ability to speak to them about the good news.

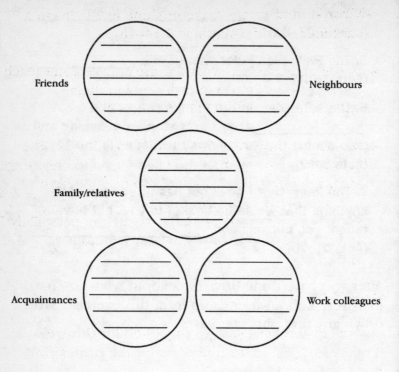

Friends

Neighbours

Family/relatives

Acquaintances

Work colleagues

Exercise Three

Here is a short Bible study you can do that involves thinking about the discoveries you have just made. The idea of this Bible study is to look at how our lives can be models for others. The exercise, however, is not designed to condemn us! Rather, we should be challenged, and made to think of our responsibility of representing Jesus and his standards in a world that has fallen so far away from him.

◆ We are God's children living in a fallen world. What kind of lives should we lead? (Philippians 2:14–15)

◆ What kind of things make us shine like lights in a darkened world? (Matthew 5:14–16)

◆ In the early church, what did the apostle Peter teach Christian wives to do in order to win their unbelieving husbands? (1 Peter 3:1–2)

◆ Read 2 Corinthians 9:6–15 and Mark 4:26–29. The Corinthian passage has often been used to encourage financial giving, but it should also be applied to evangelism. In giving out the good news, we will share the fruit of the Spirit. How can you personally, and in your own normal way, sow generously?

Daily Studies

As well as the daily studies suggested for this week, pray regularly and from now on for the names you wrote down in Exercise Two.

Also, see if you can invite one or more of the people round for a meal or a coffee, or go out for a drink at the pub or a cafe. Don't set them up—'What kind of quiche do you like, and by the way what do you think of God?!'—you are building up a friendship which God can use to reveal his love.

Make a note in your diary for early December: when you are making preparations for Christmas, have a party. Invite a few neighbours from each side of your house, and a few from across the road. Be normal and don't ram the gospel down their throats! Invite them, if they wish, to come to your carol service—and enjoy their company for its own sake.

Day one

Read Matthew 5:13–16.

Salt has certain characteristics that we are encouraged to exhibit:

◆ **Salt purifies.** It cleanses and prevents the spreading of infection and corruption.

◆ **Salt heals.** We live in a wounded world that needs healing.

◆ **Salt preserves.** It preserves from decay. It preserves good and promotes life.

◆ **Salt adds flavour.** It adds taste to life. (Note: But if *too much* salt is used it can spoil the flavour of food!)

◆ **Salt creates thirst.** It stirs a craving deep down inside.

Reflect on these characteristics of salt and pray them into your life and situation.

Prayer

Loving Father,
Lead us by your Spirit to witness to our faith
in Christ.
May what we do build up the fellowship of
his church.
May how we live speak of his word to the
world.

May what we say testify to our life in him.
So that, as we know and love him more,
others may come to know and love him too.
Amen.

Day two

Effective, healthy growth of the church is contingent upon four main kinds of outreach:

◆ **Continuous:** the church of Acts grew every day. Evangelism, too, should be continuous—it goes on all the time (Acts 2:47).

◆ **Congregational:** Jesus sends each one of us and gives the Holy Spirit to help us (John 20:21). Evangelism should be congregational, with the whole church mobilized.

◆ **Caring:** Paul showed great care and gentleness (1 Thessalonians 2:7–8). Evangelism should be caring, demonstrated by love and sensitivity to people's needs.

◆ **Conserving:** Paul's desire was to see Christians grow into maturity (Colossians 1:28–29). Evangelism should be conserving, reflecting our desire for each new believer to grow spiritually and become active in the life of the church.

Prayer

Pray that in your church, evangelism will be continuous, congregational, caring and conserving.

Father, bless my church today in its evangelism. Help me never to give up in the spreading of your word; may each person in the church be inspired and equipped to evangelize; send me the Holy Spirit that I may love as you loved, and help me to ensure that all those who give their lives to you find a secure place in your family to serve you faithfully, through Jesus Christ our Lord. Amen.

Day three

Read Luke 6:46–49.

In this well-known passage, Jesus makes it clear that it is the wise person who builds on the rock of the word of God. During this course you have been hearing a lot about the natural evangelism that passes from friend to friend.

Spend a few moments today listening quietly to what God is saying to you in all of this. How does he want to use you in your natural evangelism?

Think about the names you wrote down in Exercise Two. During this time of quiet see if there are any names that the Lord particularly underlines. Be wise and build today on the word God has given you!

Prayer

Spend some time in prayer for your friends and contacts who are not Christians.

Dear Lord, thank you for all the friends who
have encouraged me in my faith, and in
whom I have seen the light of Jesus.
Thank you that your word makes it clear
that Christ lives in me and he wishes to
reveal himself through me to my friends,
through how I live and through the words I
say.
Please forgive me for the times I have failed
to honour you in my words and in my life,
and give me boldness and love to share my
faith with others who have yet to find you.
Through Jesus Christ my Lord. Amen.

Day four

Once there was a bachelor psychiatrist, who travelled
around giving a lecture entitled 'Ten Commandments
for Parents'. Then he married and he and his wife had
their first child. He changed the title of his lecture to
'Ten Suggestions for Parents'. In due course, the
second child arrived and he changed the title again—
this time, to 'Ten Hints for Parents'. When the third
child came along he gave up lecturing!

Spend some time today considering and praying for
your own family: parents, brothers, sisters, partners
and children.

First, take a look at a number of verses from a
variety of books from the Bible: Exodus 20:12; Psalm
90:16; Romans 12:9–19; Ephesians 4:32. Then, take
these Bible truths to pray for yourself and your family.

Prayer

Dear Lord, please give me the grace to have your strength and enabling power in fulfilling my God-given roles in the family, and from this day to build a family relationship that will be honouring to Christ and a living testimony to those who are unbelievers. Amen.

Day five

Read Philippians 1:1–30.

The apostle Paul could so easily have been discouraged about his circumstances. God has used him widely, and now he is in chains and confined to prison in Rome. Whether he will die or not he does not know, but if death does come he will rejoice in the presence of Christ. If he remains, he will continue to serve God as best he can. And continue to serve God he did! He was inspired to write some letters like Ephesians, Philippians, Colossians and Philemon. And the guards became his mission field.

◆ Was Paul restricted? Yes.

◆ Was Paul limited? Yes.

◆ Was Paul surrounded by opportunities? Yes.

The apostle Paul's attitude and example should humble us and encourage us to imitate him (1 Corinthians 4:16).

What are your circumstances? Are they difficult or easy? If they are difficult, remember Paul, who even in prison still evangelized. Whatever your situation, pray that the Spirit will give you boldness to use the opportunities given for sharing the good news.

Prayer

And this is my prayer, that your love may abound more and more in knowledge and depth of insight, so that you may be able to discern what is best and may be pure and blameless until the day of Christ, filled with the fruit of righteousness that comes through Jesus Christ—to the glory and praise of God.

Philippians 1:9–11

Day six

Read again 1 Corinthians 12:12–30.

The word 'ministry' comes from the Greek word *diakonos* meaning 'one who serves'. The word 'laity' comes from the Greek word 'Laos' meaning 'the people of God'.

In the passage from Corinthians, Paul emphasizes that it is the whole body which is given gifts for ministry, not just selected parts. Think and write about how you may learn to be a servant and continue to serve faithfully (and remember, God has called us to be faithful, not successful!).

Prayer

First, remember to pray for your friends!

> *Lord, every day this week I have offered up
> the names of my friends to you. But I want to
> go on showing them the seeds of your loving
> concern, long beyond today and tomorrow.
> Please keep showing me how to act—I know
> it is the follow-through that counts. For Jesus'
> sake. Amen.*

Then, consider the following prayer from Evelyn
Underhill. After you have done so, rest with 'The Good
Shepherd', and spend time talking to him and listening
to him about this course.

> *We offer ourselves, one way or another, to try
> to work for God. We want, as it were, to be
> among the sheepdogs employed by the Good
> Shepherd. Have you ever watched a good
> sheepdog at work? He is not an emotional
> animal. He goes on with his job quite
> steadily; takes no notice of bad weather,
> rough ground, or his own comfort. He
> seldom or never stops to be stroked. Yet his
> faithfulness and intimate communion with
> his master are one of the loveliest things in
> the world. Now and then he looks at the
> shepherd. And when the time comes for rest,
> they are generally to be found together. Let
> this be the model of your love. Amen.*

Evelyn Underhill

Answers to Exercise One:

1. his brother Simon

2. Nathaniel

3. her neighbours

4. his ex-colleagues

5. his family

6. from house to house

7. from house to house

CHAPTER 4

How can I share my story?

I love hearing people's stories. So does everyone else, because what are the most popular magazines? People magazines. What are the most popular programmes on TV? Soap operas. And what do we do all day long, given half a chance? Gossip about people!

We in the West have been fairly good at stating and explaining the gospel truth through theological propositions, sometimes even using logical or scientific processes to 'prove' it. We are now beginning to realize what many of the Christians in the East have known all along—that major and important truths are also communicated through metaphor and allegory—in other words through storytelling.

The Bible is not just a book of stories, of course, but it does use the story form as a way of communicating the good news. Jesus himself is the greatest exemplar of this. He told stories about people in real life situations, and because he was always alert to the needs of others, these stories always held some particular truth for those he was talking to.

Jesus spoke all these things to the crowd in parables; he did not say anything to them without using a parable.
Matthew 13:34

In fact, Jesus seldom spoke to people at all *without* telling a story. He knew that they desperately needed to have personal knowledge of certain truths, and that parables were by far the most effective way to communicate these truths. For him, gospel-telling and story-telling were inextricably bound together. What we need to do today is to tell God's story, and our story, and simply show how the two intersect.

The gospel message needs to be communicated in three parts:

1. Telling his story—God's story from Genesis through to the life, death and resurrection of Jesus Christ.

2. Telling your story—which illustrates God's story and his power in your life.

3. Telling their story—how God's story relates to the person you are witnessing to.

Come and listen, all you who fear God; let me tell you what he has done for me.
Psalm 66:16

In this chapter, we will concentrate on number 2— telling your story.

Getting the story straight

There are various points about getting the story straight. The first is made clear in John's Gospel, when Jesus heals a man born blind. Afterwards, the man is brought before the Pharisees who are endeavouring to find fault with Jesus; but the cured man says he refuses to be drawn. He says:

> *Whether he is a sinner or not, I don't know. One thing I do know. I was blind, but now I see.*
> **John 9:25**

We need to notice this response. It is very important to your own story, particularly if you feel (along with the rest of the human race!) that your grasp of arguments for the Christian faith is sometimes very poor. At the very least, you, too, can say, 'one thing I do know...'

We have a natural desire to tell our story, but let's be truthful about it and not pretend to have all sorts of answers when we don't. Another way to be straight is to recognize the following:

> *For we cannot help speaking about what we have seen and heard.*
> **Acts 4:20**

The background to this verse is that Peter and John have been brought before the Sanhedrin (who were the Jewish Supreme Court), who in turn have commanded the apostles 'not to speak or teach at all in the name of Jesus' (Acts 4:18). And the disciples basically reply, 'We can't help it!'

We also see this pattern in the life of the apostle Paul. On one occasion he was brought before King Herod Agrippa II. The king gave Paul permission to speak for himself and Paul gave a personal testimony of what God had done in his life (Acts 26:1–29).

In his impassioned account, Paul behaves both like a witness and a lawyer. There is a big difference between the two: according to the dictionary, a lawyer pleads the case for others, taking all the facts and pressing for a decision in order to get a judgment of 'yes' or 'no'; a witness, on the other hand, is 'a person who testifies to events or facts within their own knowledge'. In other words, 'this is what I know'.

An evangelist is like a lawyer, and although God has not called all of us to be 'lawyers' for him he has called us all to be 'witnesses'—'this is what I know'. And nobody is a better authority on what happened to you than you!

But while we have a great story to tell, we must make sure we have the story straight, so that others can understand us. We also need to listen carefully to other people's particular need, so that we can relate the right part of the story to meet their need.

Why do people receive Christ into their lives?

I was once talking with a group of students, and I got that old thorny comment, 'Ah, but all religion is a crutch!'

And I thought to myself, though I didn't say it, 'In some ways, I hope you break your leg!'

The reason why people invite Jesus into their lives is because they *need* him. We all do. If that student were to break his leg, he would soon come to see what a wonderful aid a crutch is at a time of considerable distress. I am a broken person. I *need* Jesus to restore me to wholeness with God. If we're honest about it, every single person on this earth needs God desperately in today's world. This, too, can be part of both your story and theirs.

Why does Jesus' way work?

Jesus always seemed to be doing two things: asking questions and telling stories. Many Christians seem to be doing two other things: giving answers and 'preaching'!

All four may be important and necessary—explained in the right way, in the right place and at the right time! However, we tend to forget that the God of the Bible was a very good communicator, and we ignore Jesus' example at our peril.

When Jesus told parables, he always started with a need, a hurt, an interest. Often his messages were in response to questions. He scratched where people itched instead of what we so often do—pounce in with answers and sermonettes before the listener is ready and open to hear. Really good stories scratch where you itch; they don't bash you over the head with a hammer!

Putting first things first

One thing our story will depend on is knowing the Lord and experiencing his presence in our lives. That is the good news. It's not as though we are running around trying to give people some disease. We know the solution to the very thing that people need deep down. But it is important to remember that many of us are only called to be witnesses, not lawyers. So don't worry so much about preaching the gospel as *being* the gospel!

When John Wesley was asked, 'Why do people seem to be so drawn to you, almost like a magnet?' He replied, 'Well, you see, when you set yourself on fire, people just love to come and see you burn.' This is true 'overflow evangelism'; not just a programme, but a fire within. Michael Green notes this in his book, *Evangelism—Now and Then*:

> *Today's church is full of methods of evangelism, but not a great deal gets done. There is not enough fire in the belly. Once the fire is there, people discover the methods.*

As we keep drinking from the wells of salvation others will be drawn to the warmth of God's fire within us, even though they may not at first be able to name its source. We must continually stoke and feed the fire— and our own story—through prayer, Bible study and fellowship, as we are being transformed by the presence of his Holy Spirit.

Different kinds of stories

It is important to see that we all have more than one story to tell. As well as our conversion story we also have another story to tell whenever God answers our prayer and does something in our lives.

One of my prayer partners, Phyllis, who is now over seventy, rang me recently to tell me six stories of God's goodness and faithfulness the previous week!

Four parts to our personal story

While there are obviously variations, everyone's story breaks down into roughly four areas. You will write about them when you are doing the exercises later; for now, just allow the following to simmer at the back of your mind:

◆ My life before I became a Christian.

◆ How I realized I needed Jesus Christ.

◆ How I committed my life to Christ.

◆ What it means to me now.

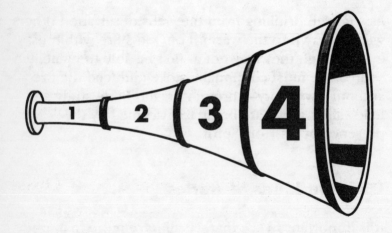

Part 1: My life before I was a Christian

I can't remember the day I was born, but I was, because there seems to be evidence to suggest it! And, for me, there was definitely a part of my life which took place before I became a Christian. For others, too, who were not Christians earlier in life, the question is this: how would we describe our attitudes, behaviour and feelings about before we became Christians?

On the other hand, you may feel that there was no part of your life before you were a Christian, because you were brought up in a Christian family and so you have always known the Lord. But I would suggest that for many, many people, if not all, there has nevertheless been a point—Christian upbringing or no Christian upbringing—even if it was very early in life, when you 'twigged': a moment when you said something like, 'Aha! This means something, and I want to take it on board!'

In fact, it is not whether or not we have had a conversion experience that counts in proving that we are Christians. What counts is evidence to show we *are now* in a relationship with Jesus. So for those brought up in the Christian faith the question is this: how would you sum up your early period of Christian understanding?

Part 2: How I realized I needed Jesus Christ

For those who were not Christians, *why* did you become a Christian? What was your story? And what precisely was the reason that you turned to Jesus at that specific time in your story? Was it because of the truth you suddenly understood about him? Or because of his forgiveness and healing? Or his comfort from loneliness? His promise of new hope, new life?

And for those already brought up as Christians, what made you realize that what you were born into and brought up to believe was really true, and *you* really believed it?

One of the most powerful tools we have in helping others is to enable them to understand why we, living in the twentieth century, have committed our lives to someone who was born 2,000 years ago! We need to communicate something about why this commitment took place, and that it is to a *living* person, who is eternal. We have become Christians because of who Jesus is, and what he did on our behalf by dying on a cross.

Part 3: How I committed my life to Jesus

Some years ago, a somewhat seedy BBC producer was visiting Paraguay, where she stayed briefly at a reservation of 1,000 Lengua Indians.
Impressively run by themselves, the reservation produced enough income from its farming and weaving for all its needs, including a school, a church and a health clinic. It was, however, helped by a Dutch missionary couple, Peter and Ianni, who were the accountant and agriculturalist for the reservation.

The producer was puzzled by the missionaries' lack of apparent zeal. A simple grace had been said over supper, but there seemed to be no other evidence of their Christian commitment. They seemed, on the contrary, to be far more concerned with how to make the best of Paraguayan trade tariffs, how to get the reservation's jeep back on the road (spare parts were always 'lost' at customs) and how to get more serum for snake-bites.

On further questioning, the producer found out that the Bibles were in Lengua, as were the church services, and the missionary couple (who only spoke Spanish) took no part in officiating at any of them.

So what, asked the producer, was the point of them being there?

They both laughed and, still smiling, Peter explained patiently that preaching and officiating did not make you a Christian missionary. Being Christian did. Had the producer thought about being a Christian, he asked?

And for the first time in her life, the producer said, 'Yes.'

Where and how did you enter into a relationship with Jesus? Was it gradual? Or was it at a specific place and time? Were any steps taken in entering this relationship for you? Alexander Solzhenitsyn was in prison. I was kneeling in my bedroom in my home in London, reading a booklet called 'Journey into Life'. Others have seen a wonderful example in someone else, and have claimed a new relationship with Jesus for themselves as a result. Others again have come forward at an evangelistic meeting. What about you?

Part 4: What it means to me now

What difference has it made to you becoming a Christian? What are the benefits? How has it affected your attitudes, emotions, actions? From your experience of being a Christian why would you encourage others to turn to Christ?

Personal experience is not just a last resort when we are stuck for argument. It is a very powerful and practical back-up for all we are saying. It shows that this is not just theory, this is real, this works. It has practical effects in everyday life.

We need to think through our story and highlight various parts of it that we could use for others. When you work through the exercise at the end of this chapter, it will be helpful to spend most time on Part 2 and Part 4.

Elements in stories that *don't* work

There are lots of things that can put people off when you're telling a story! Not paying attention to the needs of the person with you is always at the top of the list, but there are plenty of variations on this!

◆ First, don't play the game of my-story-is-better-than-yours. You know how your heart sinks when the person you are expressing your needs to suddenly says, 'Oh, how awful for you, but let me tell you how bad / terrible / difficult / exciting / holy I felt when that happened to *me*...' Your story only serves God when it serves another's need.

◆ Be honest, and don't exaggerate! Sometimes we have a tendency to blow things out of proportion. It has been said by some, 'Come to Jesus and he will solve all your problems.' It is more honest to say,

'Without Jesus Christ our problems cannot be ultimately solved.' What Jesus gives us is the integrity to carry things through.

Let's be careful we don't promise things even Jesus didn't promise! I actually find the more honest I am the more open people are. Of course my children are not immune to chicken pox, of course they get colds; we still have to pay the mortgage, and the car still breaks down. Such things, if I'm honest, help others to say, 'Hey, he's just like me!' The difference is that I now have a strength and peace to cope with these situations and problems. I have a different security. God has added a new dimension to my life.

I sometimes even talk about my fears and confusion and frustration at not understanding. I say, quite truthfully, that I don't understand why some people have accidents, or suffer from famines and injustice; but, despite these questions, I do know who holds the key to my life.

◆ Avoid negative remarks about other religions and denominations. We do not need to put other religions down to lift Jesus up. Jesus is unique. Interweave his story (which is 'history') and my story (which is a mystery!). If, however, there are genuine questions about other religions then we may comment, but lovingly; and if we do not have an answer, we can go and do some homework and talk again on another occasion.

One story I sometimes tell is about a person who is going down a road and she's not absolutely certain of the way. The going gets trickier, and after a while she comes to a fork in the road. She could go left, or she could go right, and she doesn't know which way is best.

At this point she notices two people lying in the street. One is lying facing the left fork and the other is facing the right one. They both look as if they know the way, but there's one important difference between them. One's dead, and one's alive. Which one would you ask for direction?

♦ Take great care how you use Bible references:

For the Word of God is living and active, sharper than any double-edged sword, it penetrates even to dividing soul and spirit, joints and marrow, it judges the thoughts and attitudes of the heart.
Hebrews 4:12

Don't carry a large black Bible! Jesus often quoted briefly from the Old Testament, and I have often found that a story from the Bible or a verse *is* 'living and active, sharper than any double-edged sword.' But how often we are tempted to hurl one verse after another. We get so excited by our great big harvest, we forget we are meant to be sowing seeds. One or two verses and a great deal of silence will win more people to the love of God than almost any amount of spouting—remember how Jesus criticized the Pharisee for doing just that.

♦ Don't use religious clichés or jargon. When you write your own story later in this chapter, you can check on this. I know many preachers who speak in an unknown tongue every week and they are not even charismatic! The trouble is, the longer we are

Christians the more we pick up on religious terminology, and we tend to forget that others can just switch off at some of our language.

The first time I went to church was in 1975. I was newly interested in Christianity and keen to discover more. But in the prayers we were asked to pray for Concorde. My mind flipped. What had happened to the plane? Had it crashed? What a calamity! It was only after the service, when I said I hadn't realised that something had happened to the new plane, that someone else explained that they had been praying for people getting on well together—concord.

The apostle Paul says in 1 Corinthians 2:1, 'As for me, brothers, when I came to you it was not with any show or oratory or philosophy, but simply to tell you what God had guaranteed.' Notice the word 'simply'! Simple does not mean shallow. Simple does not mean superficial. The strongest things in life are the simplest things in life. The Christian message is simple and Satan loves to complicate the gospel.

◆ Don't be long-winded. Some people sometimes go into a lot of details which are really unnecessary. 'It was 9 February, a Friday, no, it was a Saturday, in the afternoon, in fact it was early evening and I was on my way, no, actually I was getting ready to go… ' This is so *frustrating*! The shorter it is the more effective it can be. Just tell the story, simply and naturally, it's far better!

Remember, too, that we are frequently only required to share a segment of the orange, not the whole orange, a part of the story, not the whole story. Sometimes it will be appropriate to share two segments of the story or three or four—perhaps, once in a while, the whole story. But it's worth remembering what one farmer said, 'When I feed my cows I don't give them a whole bale of hay!'

◆ Finally, when you are telling a story, let God do the growing. In Acts 17 the apostle Paul addressed a meeting of the Areopagus. After listening to him 'some of them sneered but others said, "we want to hear you again on this subject"' (verse 32). In other words, some were interested. They were made to think. They didn't hear and then instantly become Christians, but said they would like to hear more.

When we are witnessing to others and sharing our story, it may be good to say, 'Well, we have probably talked enough for now, if you're interested we could talk again some other time,' and let God take over.

You will make, as I do, many mistakes. But let us have a humble boldness and trust in the living God and we will not go far wrong if we take for ourselves God's words to Paul in Acts:

> *Do not be afraid, keep on speaking, do not be silent. For I am with you.*
> **Acts 18:9**

Exercise One

On a fresh page in your notebook, make two columns. In the first column, list the various needs that people frequently have. In the second column, write the solutions that Jesus offers to them.

EXAMPLE

Problem	**What Jesus Christ offers**
Feeling lonely	Friendship, the closest of all relationships
Scared of criticism	Reassurance, courage

Think of the people you know who have yet to meet Jesus. Be careful *not* to decide for them whether or not they have problems but, instead, commit yourself simply to asking one person this week what his or her problems may be. If the person decides to confide in you, ask if you can help in practical ways.

Exercise Two

This exercise is designed to help you tell your own story. If that seems a little self-indulgent, you may be having some fears about your own self-worth. If you are, you need to look back at the verification process in Chapter 1 and find out if your mind is lying! Everyone is of unique and priceless value to God—you included!

Remember, too, that you are putting together your story to use it for witnessing. When you have written it, if you are concerned about how your story sounds you could try it out first with someone from your church who is willing to help you be clear. If, for example, you find yourself using a lot of clichés, it is important to be challenged—gently, of course!

Part 1—My life before I was a Christian

◆ What problems or difficult situations were you facing?

◆ Where was life unsatisfactory for you?

Part 2—How I realized I needed Jesus Christ

◆ What caught your attention?

◆ What was it about Jesus that attracted you to him?

Part 3—How I committed my life to Jesus Christ

◆ Where were you?

◆ What specifically did you do?

◆ What did you pray?

Part 4—What it means to me now

◆ What difference has it made?

◆ What are the costs?

◆ What are the benefits?

Once you have completed this section, tell your story to yourself again, based on the notes you have made. Assume you are talking to someone who is not a Christian.

A good place to try this out is in the bath! But if you really find it impossible to tell your own story to yourself, see if you can find a willing Christian friend this week on whom you can try it out.

Spend some time in prayer, thanking God for the story he has given you, and asking him to bless this story greatly, that others may come to Christ as a result of hearing it.

Exercise Three

Write down how you think *you*, with your natural gifts and qualities, can be Jesus' hands for others? How can you share with them the solutions Jesus offers in a loving, non-aggressive way? If you are troubled by fears about a lack of self-worth as you do this, deal with them first, again by using the verification process in Chapter 1. God will enable you to act, and act well, if you give him half a chance!

Pray for those friends who came to mind in Chapter 3. Pray particularly that you will be given opportunity to speak to them this week.

Exercise Four

Don't get me wrong: much ritual and language in the Christian tradition is extremely helpful to those who deeply understand it. Everything from icons, incense, bells and elaborate clothing to highly symbolic language can support worship and faith in a mystical and wonderful way. But to those outside faith, they can be a bigger switch-off than almost anything else. So when you evangelize, speak plainly. To help you do this, write what *you* mean, in plain English, by the following ten terms:

sacrament; saved; salvation; blood of the lamb; 'Praise the Lord'; hallelujah; hosanna; Amen; kingdom; host.

Add any other words you personally have had problems with, and explain these too.

Exercise Five

Look through the following questions that some people have used as objections to the Christian faith. See if you can find out some answers and write them down. (You will find a list of books which may help at the end of this chapter.)

◆ How can you believe in a God of love if there is so much suffering in the world?

◆ Don't all religions lead to God?

◆ Isn't the Bible full of contradictions?

◆ What about those people who have never heard about Jesus—do they go to hell?

Exercise Six

We all have lots of different stories. It is helpful to identify them so that when we are speaking to someone we can share the most appropriate story to their situation. It might be a story about God's healing or his provision. It might be about the restoration of a bad relationship, or an experience of peace in a difficult situation. Spend some time this week making a note of any stories from the past couple of years, and keep a note so that you can use them as and when the Holy Spirit prompts you.

Resources

The Day Death Died, Michael Green (IVP)
Dead Sure?, J. John (IVP)
Is Anyone There?, David Watson (Hodder and Stoughton)
Why We Can't Believe, Paul Weston (IVP)

Daily Studies

Day one

In the book of Acts, chapters 6 and 7, we find that despite opposition the church in Jerusalem had grown at an amazing rate. From the small beginnings in chapter 1, to 3,000 in chapter 2, to 5,000 in chapter 4, to 'multitudes', both men and women, in chapter 5. And in chapter 6:7 we read that: *the number of the disciples increased rapidly*.

At this stage God is preparing to expand the frontiers of the church's mission into Judea and Samaria. This week we will look at how the church in Acts grew. The events of chapters 6 to 8 describe how these frontiers have expanded.

The whole passage is dominated by the life, ministry and death of Stephen—the first Christian leader to lay down his life for Jesus, and the man who we will be learning from for much of this week.

Read Acts 6:8–15. Re-read verse 15.

Howard Marshall in his commentary on Acts writes:

> *The description is of a person who is close to God and reflects some of his glory as a result of being in his presence.*

One word which Luke repeatedly uses to describe Stephen is the word 'full'.

Read Acts 6:5, Acts 6:8 and Acts 7:55.

Stephen is a man who is just full of God! He is an example of what being filled with the Holy Spirit produces. This is very significant, because the person you are determines the work God will do.

Thank the Lord for Stephen and pray that we may be men and women full of faith, God's grace and God's Holy Spirit.

Prayer

> *Grant, O Lord, that what we have*
> *said with our lips,*
> *we may believe in our hearts and*
> *practise in our lives;*
> *and in your mercy keep us faithful*
> *unto the end;*
> *for Jesus Christ's sake. Amen.*

Day two

Read Acts 6:8–15. Re-read verse 10.

There is a remarkable strength of character about Stephen. His angel face (verse 15) means anything but weakness, and he towers over his accusers. His wisdom (verse 10) is not academic—it's not something to be had from books and study. It is the fulfilment of Jesus' promise in Luke:

> *I will give you words and wisdom that none of your adversaries will be able to resist or contradict.*
> **Luke 21:15**

What is the secret of this wisdom?

Read Psalm 119:97–100.

The most obvious conclusion one can draw from Acts 7 is that Stephen was also filled with holy scriptures. It just pours out of him, for his heart and mind were steeped in it. We need to be students of the Bible. Pray that God will renew your appetite for his word.

> *The appetite grows with eating.*
> **French proverb**

Commit yourself to a regular study of the Bible so that, in Charles Spurgeon's words:

> *Our very blood may become 'bibline.'*

Prayer

Dear Lord, inspire us by your Holy Spirit to read, understand and apply your word to our lives. May your word strengthen and nourish us that we may bless others with words of life. Amen.

Day three

Stephen's ministry is so important that a whole chapter (Acts 7), the longest in the book of Acts, is devoted to it. The thing which made Stephen's ministry so effective was the power of God which was upon and in him.

There are two main themes running through Stephen's speech and they correspond to the two charges made against him.

Read Acts 6:11 and 13.

Stephen's speech to the Sanhedrin is a script on mission, taking in the whole scope of the Old Testament. He draws a straight line from Abraham to Christ and sees the whole of biblical history as the unfolding purpose of God preparing the way for Jesus. Read Acts 7:1–53.

Stephen was a messenger who presented the truth of God. Think about this person who both loved God's word, and was also so open to the power of the Spirit.

Prayer

Pray that as our appetite for God's word grows, so also our openness to God's Spirit will grow, that we might boldly share God's story with other people.

> *O make me understand it, help me to take it in.*
> *What it meant to thee, the holy one, to bear away my sin. Amen.*

Day four

Stephen was a martyr who laid down his life for the glory of God (Acts 7:54–58).

Read Acts 7:54–8:1.

There are two sides to Stephen's death: on the one hand is the fury of the council, described in verse 54, and on the other is the glory of God in verses 55–56. Stephen's death also introduces us, in verse 58, to the figure who is going to dominate the rest of the book of Acts. This was Saul of Tarsus who was to become Paul, the apostle to the gentiles.

Stephen dies after just one sermon. Was his life prematurely cut off and thrown away before its time had come? No! His life was the fuel which set alight a flame for the glory of God in the ancient world that has no parallel!

If you or I had been Stephen, having delivered such a powerful sermon we might have liked to see at least a few people fall to their knees and become Christians.

But apparently there were no conversions and Stephen could have been quite dejected. But he wasn't, because his peace came from being obedient to his master rather than from seeing results.

Much of our evangelism will seem unproductive. We will explain the gospel, tell our story, sense the power of the Spirit, and there might seem to be little evidence of the other person being touched by God. But, like Stephen, we will need to develop that discipline of faithfully sowing the seed of God's word in the power of the Spirit, and leaving the results to God. Who knows what 'Saul of Tarsus' might be nearby, listening to your conversation?

Prayer

Heavenly Father, thank you for the example of Stephen who humbled himself to wait at tables, yet who was also given such a wonderful vision of your glory.
Grant me that same grace, to love you and your word so much that, being empowered by your Spirit, I may be freely available to you as a messenger of your word. Please use me today to share the good news of your Son with someone who has yet to meet him.
Amen.

Spend some time praying for those friends whose names you wrote down earlier. Listen to the Spirit—is he calling you to speak to any of them? Perhaps he will reveal a particular insight about one of them, and what

God wants you to do. Be open to the Spirit's promptings today.

Day five

Read Acts 13:1–3.

It was while the church at Antioch was worshipping and fasting that the Holy Spirit said,

Set apart for me Barnabas and Saul, for the work to which I have called them.

Worship and evangelism are bound together. The reason for this is because worship is giving glory to God. So if we are worshipping God and desiring his glory, can we be unmoved by the fact that there are areas of our country and world where God is not being glorified? That is one reason why worship and evangelism go together. In worship and evangelism, God is glorified.

In the last century, Henry Martyn, a Cambridge scholar, turned his back on academic glory to go to India. In India he watched people bowing and prostrating before pagan images and he heard someone tell of a vision they had of Jesus bowing before an idol. Henry Martyn wrote:

I was cut to the soul at this blasphemy. I could not endure existence if Jesus was not glorified; it would be hell to me if he were thus dishonoured.

Today, many in the church have lost this deeply felt emotion for the glory of God. Spend some time now in worship and, as you glorify God, allow your heart to be moved for the lost. Ask the Holy Spirit to pray through you for the world. As the Spirit stirs in you in worship and intercessory prayer for the lost in the world, you may well begin to feel some of the deep places in the heart of God.

> *We do not know what we ought to pray, but the Spirit himself intercedes for us with groans that words cannot express.*
> **Romans 8:26**

Prayer

Say this prayer slowly line by line. Allow the Spirit to move in you.

> *Come, Holy Spirit.*
> *Come and move in my heart.*
> *Come and pray through me for the lost.*
> *Come and give me again a vision of the glory of God.*
> *Stir in me a longing to see God glorified.*
> *Father, Son and Holy Spirit I worship you.*
> *Holy is your name. Amen.*

Day six

Read Acts 16:6–10.

The apostles found themselves being sent not so much to people they had chosen, as to people God had chosen for them. Time and time again, their own inclinations were corrected either by direct divine intervention or by God-created circumstances.

In Acts 16:6–8, Paul and his team experience one frustration after another. Doors were closing against them rather than opening, confounding their plans rather than fulfilling them. They had to learn to die to their own plans for the sake of God's plans; to die to their own timetable in order to live by God's.

Have you experienced frustration in trying to share the good news in places where you thought it was obvious to share it? Perhaps God has been closing some doors, in order to channel you in the right direction.

Spend some time asking the Lord to show you where the right mission field is. Listen to the promptings of the Spirit.

Can you sense 'a man from Macedonia' calling you? Is God showing you someone who is longing to hear the good news, who needs you to go to them? If you do feel God is directing you to someone, then pray that the way will be made clear for you to meet with them today or at least very soon.

Prayer

Father, I abandon myself into your hands.
Do with me what you will.
Whatever you may do, I thank you.
I am ready for all, I accept all.
Let only your will be done in me. Amen.

Charles de Foucauld

CHAPTER 5

How do social concern and evangelism go together?

When you think of the life of Christ, it is extremely hard to understand how evangelism and social concern could *not* go together. Perhaps the glitzy publicity given to a few television evangelists over the last decade or so has suggested otherwise—that evangelism is only about over-enthusiastic preaching rather than social action. In reality, however, nothing is, or should be, further from the truth.

Tale of Two Boys

Stomachs protruding, bulging, sore. Two reasons: 'Mum, can I have more turkey?' 'Help yourself, there's plenty more.'

'Mum, isn't there anything to eat? My stomach's sore.' 'Maybe tomorrow.'

One mum laughs, the other mum cries. Inflation's cutting the pay cheque. We will have to economize. Drought ravaged land. No game. No grain. One dad trying to keep his standard alive. The other struggling to survive.

'I don't like sweet potatoes.' 'Well there's plenty of mashed.'

'Dad, could you find anything to eat?'

'Nothing.'

Now thank we all our God. *'You know I don't like pumpkin pie.' 'Then eat the meat.' 'I don't like that either.' 'Surprise! I baked a cherry pie just for you.'*

'Nothing, nothing. It's been three days. Maybe tomorrow.'

'Mum, my stomach hurts.' 'That's what you get for eating like a pig. Quieten down. You won't die. Dad's getting some Alka Seltzer.'

'Mum, my stomach hurts.' 'I know son, maybe tomorrow there'll be something. Dad's out looking.'

Stomachs protruding, bulging sore. Two boys. Two reasons. One is stuffed the other is starved.

Social justice

Social justice can be promoted quite separately from Christianity. After the World War II, it was the driving cause and primary function of the new welfare state and it continues to be the core basis for humanitarian charities all over the world, Christian and secular. The only problem is that without the good news of God's compassionate love, 'social justice' can become the arid call of just another group of dissidents: the strident voice of the angry left-wing council, the bitter demand of the jobless, forlorn of hope and full of pessimistic resentments.

Likewise, Christianity can be promoted quite separately from social justice, arguably with even more disastrous results. Not only do those who loudly proclaim the gospel while doing little about it give God a bad name, such individuals are no more 'faith-full' than the Pharisee on the street corner or the wealthy philanthropist who tells tramps to get lost.

For both truly to fulfil God's word, social justice and Christian evangelism must be integral parts of one another. Together they combine the 'works' and the 'faith' without which neither means very much. Evangelism in its biblical sense is concerned both with a person's relationship to God and with his or her relationships and responsibilities to other people.

Social justice can also be a link. It can go before the gospel-telling part of evangelism, because it can open closed doors, break down prejudice, and be a bridge across which the gospel may pass. Once people's 'felt needs' are clearly the area of your concern, their 'spiritual needs' may reveal themselves and the Holy Spirit may begin his work.

Christ's reasons for social justice

But even if no bridge were created by your social actions or mine, God's people would still have a reason to concern themselves with social justice. For Jesus, conversions were of secondary importance compared to revealing the love of God in the first place. Jesus put first things first. He came to do the work his heavenly father had sent him to do, *regardless* of any so-called rewards.

> *He gave himself for us, to rescue us from all*
> *wickedness and to make us a pure people who*
> *belong to him alone and are eager to do good.*
> **Titus 2:14**

And because of this, social justice was of paramount importance to our Lord.

Now let us first be very clear about one thing: to Jesus, 'love' was not a noun; it was, and is, a verb. It isn't a nice gooey feeling, or a sweet sympathy for those in difficulty; it's an action. When someone came to their minister recently and said that he didn't know where the loving feelings had gone from his marriage, his minister pointed out that if he couldn't feel it, he should do it: clean up the house, do the shopping and ironing, take his wife out, discuss matters of importance with her; those loving feelings, he assured him, would soon come back.

Christians should be taught to observe *everything* the Lord commanded, showing their faith by their works. They are called on to *do*, not merely to feel. They must feed the hungry, visit those in prison and clothe the naked; they must struggle against everything that condemns people to a sub-human existence—hunger, disease, poverty, inequality and injustice. The church must exhibit an obvious concern for all segments of society, since all people are called to share in the kingdom. Only following on from this real and radical kind of 'purity' can the gospel be preached as a call to liberation from all that enslaves the human spirit and from all the results of individual and collective sin.

The response of Christians

At a night hostel in Oxford, not so long ago, a couple of teenagers were discussing the kindness of one of the people running the shelter.

'Yeah, it's great', said one. 'I dunno how she does it. She works in the hospital all day, then she comes here and gets us lot. Makes you wonder what makes her tick.'

'She told me she was a Christian—you know, from the church next door,' said the other.

'Nah, can't be that,' said the first. 'Their doors is closed all day every day except Sunday. Because of us.'

It is clearly not Sunday churchgoing that convinces unbelievers about the goodness of God's kingdom; on the contrary. Nor, even, is it meaningful words and statements outside church on Sunday. What makes an impact is positive programmes designed to better the condition of the disadvantaged and neglected. It is these that are the indispensable parts of evangelism and that must receive the fullest support of the whole church, and of *each person in the church* as they are able.

If we need proof of this fact beyond what we are instructed to do in the Bible, there are plenty of other indicators. For instance, an international research organization recently conducted a worldwide survey on leaders who make a difference and whom you cannot ignore. Two names came at the top of the list: Mother Teresa and Archbishop Desmond Tutu. Compassion and justice are the real language that the world understands.

Why does poverty exist?

Some people see poverty as a self-inflicted wound— caused by a mixture of lack of effort, mismanagement and bad luck. Other people see poverty linked to deficiencies, weaknesses and maladjustments of families, and suggest that children are trained to repeat the failure, delinquency, crime and immorality of those nearest to them—'the sins of the fathers are visited upon the next generation'. A third view is that poverty is enforced by the rich and powerful in order to maintain the status quo.

Whichever is true, you only need to multiply a few individual examples, and you begin to get a wider nightmare. A group of individuals soon form a ghetto, a ghetto soon becomes a region, and a region can soon become a whole country, even a group of countries.

In classic economic terms, a person's income reflects their competitive worth. Since people are responsible individually for their actions and conditions, monetary rewards go to those with talent and effort. But individuals are only part of a wider economic picture; and if a community's resources are run-down, even those with talent and effort may go down with it. The whole group becomes one almost doomed to material failure.

The poor: biblical perspectives

The biblical view of poverty, however, is very different from that found in government assessments and conclusions. The Old Testament uses several different Hebrew words when referring to the poor: *ani* is the most common word, used seventy-seven times. The *ani* literally means 'a person bowed down', someone who has to look up to others on whom they are dependent. It is worth noting that *ani* is contrasted not with the rich, therefore, but with the oppressor who basically keeps the *ani* in the position they are in.

A second word used to describe the poor in the Bible is *anaw*, which is used eighteen times, and refers to people who feel they have little value or worth before God. A third term, *ebyon*, is used sixty times and refers to the situation of 'beggars'.

All these words—*ani, anaw, ebyon*—are full of emotion. They are not neutral words, but are words that call for urgent change. It is interesting that the word 'poor' does not occur in the book of Genesis at all. There was no contrast between rich and poor. Abraham was the example of this unproblematic understanding of riches. In this period the riches were those of the whole 'tribe'—so if one was rich, all members of the tribe were rich.

The most common New Testament Greek word used for poor is *ptochos* which literally means 'to duck away in fear'. Someone who has to try to live completely without means and therefore is reduced to begging.

There are other words—meaning lowly, needy, insignificant, weak, simple-minded, oppressed. We also find many references to the social conditions of the time. There is talk of landowners, tax collectors, labourers, slaves, honest and dishonest stewards, creditors, unjust judges, and widows pleading for their rights. These references bring to light the extremes of rich and poor, and of those with and without power.

In itself a list doesn't indicate everything, but in the great variety of terms and expressions the Bible gives us many more meanings to the words 'rich' and 'poor' than do our modern-day institutions.

In the famous parable of the Good Samaritan, Jesus depicted life in the gutter. Through the eyes of a victim we saw the priest and the Levite passing by and the Samaritan stopping. 'Justice' was suddenly revealed as the opposite of 'just us'. The barriers were broken, and it was love that made the bridge from one tribe to another.

Sometimes the most important things we say are the things that we do for people, being concerned about the concerns of others, loving and caring for those who are unlike ourselves. The Reverend Marie Elizabeth Dyer, a hospital chaplain, writes of her experience:

> *I already knew I was not an evangelist. I did not feel called upon to baptize all nations, nor all peoples. I learned to love more deeply and to hold this commandment primary in my life. One day I was reading Matthew 25:35–36, 'for I was hungry and you gave me something to eat, I was thirsty and you gave me something to drink, I was a stranger and you invited me in. I needed clothes and you clothed me, I was sick and you looked after me. I was in prison and you came to visit me.'*

Marie began to interpret these verses in a new way because she knew the hunger, thirst, nakedness and imprisonment of her patients. So she wrote:

> *I was hungry...*
> *... for a new life away from the pressures of an alcoholic husband—you did not give me a life away, but new ways to live with my man;*

... for breath that would not make me gasp—I continued to gasp but you stayed, I knew that you cared;

... for company, for I am the only one in this room without visitors—you brought me a flower, laughed at my jokes and read scripture to me.

... I was thirsty for the knowledge of a diagnosis—you helped me to face whatever I heard;

... for righteousness, a sense of forgiveness in life—I knew that you believed and I began to believe too;

... for hope that a loved one indeed would not die—you left me with hope and promised to stay by my side.

... I was a stranger for I did not speak English—Thank you, you tried to communicate and did not just smile and then walk away.

... I had never been in a hospital before, I felt not only strange but terrified—you believed my fear, you prayed with me too.

... I was naked for I was a doctor, my inability to express feelings was exposed by your words— and you put your hand on my shoulder to tell me you knew that I cared;

... for I was old, my veins and even my bones stick out—you clothed my skin with loving caresses;

... for my grief showed all over my face—you did not avoid me, but sat down to talk.

... I was sick and you visited me.

... I was in prison in the loneliness of being unmarried—you told me you remembered the hardness of such days; in a room with no windows—together we shared...

The way God works for justice

The basis for the New Testament is the incarnation. God's solidarity is not just with words but with deeds.

He has taken upon himself the form of a servant.
Philippians 2:7

The incarnation was not and is not for 'just us', nor is the world for 'just us'. To be a Christian is to become open to the rest of the world, not as a master but as a servant.

What about the poor and the rich? Are the poor blessed and the rich evil? Of course not. What God *is* concerned with are the relationships between people, and the point is that the rich and powerful have the opportunities to break relationships and to set up oppressive systems. God is on the side of the poor because no one else is.

This does not make the poor godly. But it may be easier for the poor, who have nothing to begin with, to put their trust in the free gift of grace.

So the question for those of us who are not poor is whether we, in spite of our riches, are able to live our lives by a gospel of free grace and justice rather than by a gospel for 'just us'.

Evangelism and social action

We should never separate evangelism, and signs and wonders, from social justice. There is no competition between lighthouse keepers and lifeboat savers; all the different elements in evangelism belong together in one glorious mix, when we are working for God.

Mother Teresa once said,

We try to pray through our work by doing it with Jesus, for Jesus, to Jesus. That helps us to put our whole heart and soul into doing it. The dying, the crippled, the mentally ill, the unwanted, the unloved— they are Jesus in disguise.

Mrs Smith

The following story was written by Dr Robert Lupton, a psychologist whose Family Consultation Service operates out of a once-abandoned church in an inner city.

Mrs Smith is sixty-six. She's mildly retarded, badly overweight, twice a great grandmother and a devoted member of our church. Although she has to live with her extended family in a deplorable, overcrowded house, her buoyant spirit is undaunted. Since losing her youngest son in a senseless murder she has redirected much of her affection towards me.

'You're my buddy,' she'll say to me with a broad, snaggle-tooth grin. 'I pray for you every day.' And

then she'll give me a long bear hug. She wants to sit with me in every service and even though the smell of stale sweat and excrements is often nauseating, I am pleased to have Mrs Smith by my side.

She has often hinted—sometimes blatantly—that she would like to come home with us for a little visit. Nothing would delight her more than to have Sunday dinner with us.

But there is a conflict. It has to do with the values Peggy and I learned from childhood. We have always believed it is good stewardship to take care of our belongings, treat them with respect, and get long service from them. Our boys know, for instance, that they are not to track in mud on the carpet or sit on the furniture with dirty clothes. To invite Mrs Smith into our home means having filth and stench soil our couch, stains on my corduroy chair and stubborn, offensive odours in our living room. Unknowingly, she forces upon me conflict, a clashing of values inside me.

Preserve and maintain, conserve and protect… the words of an ethic that has served us well. And subtly, over time, these values of our culture have filtered into our theology until they have become part of it. It is increasingly difficult to separate the values of achievement from the values of the kingdom.

I thank God for Mrs Smith and the conflict she brings me. In her, more clearly than in Sunday

*School lessons or sermons, do I encounter the
Christ of scripture saying, 'inasmuch as you have
done it to the least of these, you have done it to
me.' 'Lord, please sit in my chair.'*

In the exercises later in this chapter, you will have a
chance to comment on this passage and to write down
your own responses. For now, just stop for a moment
to think of what your own conflicts might be in this
situation.

Where do we go from here?

Whatever our circumstances, we can always go
somewhere, even if it seems only one small step of the
way. Moreover, we always have God to help us do just
that. To quote Mother Teresa again, about her work in
Calcutta:

*We try to pray through our work by doing it with
Jesus, for Jesus, to Jesus. That helps us to put our
whole heart and soul into doing it. The dying, the
crippled, the mentally ill, the unwanted, the
unloved—they are Jesus in disguise.*

We have a lot to do and little time to do it but we can
still be encouraged—that is the great message of
Christianity. While no one person can change the
world, we can still change the world for one person!
The parable of the talents is not written to make us
feel depressed, but to help us see that whatever we
have can be used for the kingdom; as was said by the

eighteenth-century philosopher, Edmund Burke,

Nobody made a greater mistake than he who did nothing because he could only do a little.

We also have to do the right things, and not what people call 'displacement activity'. In other words, we need to concentrate most of our time on action rather than on preaching or administration.

I was hungry and you formed a committee to investigate my hunger. I was homeless and you filed a report on my plight. I was sick and you held a seminar on the situation of the under-privileged. You have investigated all the aspects of my plight, yet I am still hungry, homeless and sick.

Administration is important, of course, but how much time do the Gospels spend telling us about Jesus' administration? None! Jesus knew how much people love to occupy themselves with the so-called busyness of sorting out the problems of others. But he, by contrast, was utterly direct, working at the heart of need.

The Pit

A man fell into a pit and couldn't get himself out.
A subjective person came along and said, 'I feel for you, down there.'
An objective person came along and said: 'It's logical that someone would fall down there.'
A Christian Scientist came along: 'You only think that you are in a pit.'
A Pharisee said: 'Only bad people fall into a pit.'

A newspaper reporter wanted the exclusive story on this pit.

A fundamentalist said. 'You deserve your pit.'

Confucius said: 'If you would have listened to me, you would not be in that pit.'

Buddha said: 'Your pit is only a state of mind.'

A realist said: 'That's a pit.'

A scientist calculated the pressure necessary (lbs/sq.in) to get him out of the pit.

A geologist told him to appreciate the rock strata in the pit.

A tax man asked if he was paying tax on the pit.

The council inspector asked if he had a permit to dig a pit.

An evasive person came along and avoided the subject of the pit altogether.

A self-pitying person said: 'You haven't seen anything until you've seen my pit!'

A charismatic said: 'Just confess that you're not in a pit.'

An optimist said: 'Things could get worse.'

A pessimist said: 'Things will get worse!'

Jesus, seeing the man, took him by the hand and lifted him out of the pit!

Kenneth D. Filkins

Prayer

Lord, look through my eyes.
Listen through my ears.
Speak through my lips.
Act with my hands.
Walk with my feet.

Exercise One

We hear a great deal about 'the poor' in the church, and our news is full of concern for the needs of 'the poor'. In your notebooks, begin to work out what you think about this subject. Jesus said,

> *Blessed are you who are poor.*
> **Luke 6:20**

What do you mean when you speak of 'the poor'? What is your first thought, what picture do you have, when you hear the phrase 'the poor'? Who and where are 'the poor' in your area?

Please read and think about Deuteronomy 15:4–5; 7–11. After you have jotted down some thoughts, be quiet for a few moments and then pray:

> *O Lord God, you made me in your own image and redeemed me through Jesus your Son. Take away the arrogance and hatred which infect my heart and the hearts of others; break down the walls that separate us; unite us in the bonds of love; and work by your Holy Spirit through my struggle and confusion to accomplish your purposes on earth. Amen.*

Exercise Two

In this chapter, you have read the 'Tale of Two Boys', and the story about Mrs Smith by Dr Robert Lupton.

Think about, and then write down, what you would really do if Mrs Smith wanted to come to your home for Sunday dinner.

Exercise Three

Read James 2:14–18.

In Britain, 8,000 people sleep rough every night. Over one million elderly people do not see a friend or relative more than once a week. These facts are not mentioned here to make you feel guilty. They are simply examples of social injustice in Britain today.

In terms of social concern, write down what you are already doing in your life. Write down what is your church doing. Now add any ways you can support these activities more effectively.

Do you think there may be other needs in your area? Spend a few minutes just jotting down at random any new ideas you may have about the needs and possibilities for ministry with the poor as individuals, both on your own and with members of your church. Write down all the ideas—even the wildest ones. Do not worry about feasibility yet. All ideas are possibilities! Examine the list for patterns or clusters of ideas: for example, children, the bereaved, the homeless.

If you have difficulty thinking of ideas, ask yourself who in your area might be suffering from any of these: bereavement, homelessness, old age, drug and solvent abuse, injury, sickness, poverty, loneliness. Now commit yourself to finding out more about one of these problems this week.

As the apostle Paul frequently pointed out, everyone is different—none of us is called upon to do everything. It is highly likely, therefore, that you will have the experience and ability to befriend people in one particular way. Perhaps you have some particular skill which you can offer; write about it now. (And you'd be amazed at how many useful things you know! Everything can be a skill, from changing a washer on a tap, to visiting the social security offices with someone to help untangle information about benefits, to playing football with nine-year-olds, to listening to stories from long ago over several cups of tea... the list is endless!)

It may well be that the Holy Spirit is stirring you about a particular group in your area to which God wants to minister through you. Give time to waiting on God and listening to him.

When you have done this exercise, you may think it useful to share your thoughts with someone in your church, or pass it on to the leadership for their discernment. Later, if a new idea emerges as a strategy for social action, you can also offer to do some more detailed research on it.

Alternatively, are there ways you could help support one of the ministries that already exist in the church?

Let God continue to speak to you this week about this area of concern for the poor and vulnerable.

Daily Studies

Day one

Read Philippians 2:5–9.

Reflect and meditate on these verses. One hymn writer put it:

He emptied himself of all but love.

Jesus turned the world inside out—he loved rather than sought to be loved. He turned it upside down—he served rather than sought to be served. Jesus' love was a love that was willing to serve and suffer in serving.

Do not pray for easy living. Pray to be stronger men and women. Pray that we will be strong in the Lord and find strength to be the people he desires us to be. Let the Spirit show you where today you can show love and where you can serve.

Prayer

Lord, in these times when we fear we are losing hope, or feel that our efforts are futile, let us see in our hearts and minds the image of your resurrection.
Let that be the source of courage and strength. With that, and in your company, help us to face challenges and struggles against all that is born of injustice. Lord in your mercy, hear our prayer. Amen.

Day two

Read James 2:14–26.

Highlight the points that stand out to you. Spend some time asking the Lord for wisdom and grace to know what the James passage means for us today. Then, consider some of these questions:

◆ What are its implications for your life and lifestyle?

◆ Do you spend time and energy avoiding the costs and implications of loving and caring for others?

◆ What would be for you the implications of inviting 'Mrs Smith' to your home? Pray about this. Do you know a 'Mrs Smith'? Ask the Lord to show you whether you should invite her or anyone else for Sunday lunch, Monday supper, Tuesday tea, Wednesday elevenses, Thursday shopping, Friday trip to the launderette, Saturday football, none of these or all of them put together—and more!

If you have Christ in your heart, you are a missionary. If you do not have Christ in your heart, you are a field for missions.

Filomena Natividad

Prayer

Watch thou, dear Lord, with those who wake or watch or weep tonight and give thine angels charge over those who sleep. Tend thy sick ones, O Lord Christ.

> *Rest thy weary ones.*
> *Bless thy dying ones.*
> *Soothe thy suffering ones.*
> *Pity thine afflicted ones.*
> *Shield thy joyous ones.*
> *And all for thy love's sake. Amen.*
>
> **Augustine of Hippo**

Day three

Read Romans 12:1–2.

Meditate on these verses. Are there ways you conform to the pattern of this world? Invite the Lord to renew your mind today.

In AD125, Aristides, a Greek observer, wrote about the Christian church:

> *They walk in all humility and kindness, and falsehood is not found among them and they love one another. They despise not the widow and grieve not the orphan. He that has, distributes liberally to him that has not. If they see a stranger they bring him under their roof, and rejoice over him as if he were their own brother; for they call themselves brethren, not after the flesh, but after the Spirit and in God; but when one of their poor passes away from the world, and any one of them see him, then he provides for his burial according to his ability; and if they hear that any of their number is imprisoned or oppressed for the name of their Messiah, all of them provide for his needs, and if it is possible*

*that he may be delivered, they deliver him. And if
there is among them any man who is poor and
needy, and they have not an abundance of
necessaries, they fast two or three days that they
may supply the needy with their necessary food.*

Thank God for the early church and pray for our
church today and her responsibility in a needy world.

Prayer

*May the strength of God pilot us.
May the power of God preserve us.
May the wisdom of God instruct us.
May the hand of God protect us.
May the way of God direct us.
May the shield of God defend us.
May the host of God guard us against the
snares of the evil one and the temptations of
the world.
May Christ be with us.
Christ before us.
Christ in us.
Christ over us.
May thy salvation, O Lord, be always ours
this day and for evermore. Amen.*

St Patrick

Day four

Read Colossians 1:9–14.

Reflect on and pray these scriptures through.

Pause for thought:

◆ Mother Teresa decided after winning the Nobel Prize that she would not go to accept any more recognition because it interfered with her work. She knew she was not in the business of accepting prizes. She was in the business of serving the poor of Calcutta. She maintained her dedication to the cause by refusing unrelated honours.

◆ A true leader is committed to the cause and does not become the cause.

Prayer

O Lord, mercifully receive the prayers of your people who call upon you, and grant that they may know and understand what things they ought to do, and also may have grace and power faithfully to accomplish them; through Jesus Christ our Lord who lives and reigns with you and the Holy Spirit, one God, now and forever. Amen.

Day five

Read John 15:1–17.

Spend a few moments abiding in Jesus, becoming
aware of his love. If you like to use your imagination,
see yourself as a branch drawing strength and life from
the true vine. Feel his love and power rising in you, as
sap rises in the spring.

In Exercise Two, you spent some time thinking about
new areas to help God mete out social justice. Often,
this exercise makes us feel guilty: we aren't doing
enough, we should be better, we should be more
loving, we're no good. If you felt that, I hope you
promptly stopped it—guilt is, by and large, a misery
trap! The point of Exercise Two was to open our eyes
and notice, be aware of, be alert to, the part we can
play in the needs of our world. No more, and no less.

In fact, if you are reading this book at all, it is highly
likely that you are already active in God's programme
for social justice. Spend some time thinking about the
fruit you do bear for God—and don't go all modest!
Thank him for what he is able to do through you.

Next, listen to him. Are there ways he can help you
do this work? Is there other fruit he wants you to bear
through doing this work in new ways?

And finally, pray for God's eyes to see what we can
pray and do today—for a relative, a friend, a stranger
or an enemy.

Prayer

Grant that we may walk as Christ walked;
Grant that what the Spirit was in him, such
he may be also in us;
Grant that our lives may be re-fashioned
after the pattern of his life;
Grant that we may do today here on earth
what Christ would have done, and in the
way he would have done it;
Grant that we may become vessels of his
grace, instruments of his will.
To thy honour and glory; through Jesus Christ
our Lord. Amen.

J. H. Jowett

Day six

Read Psalm 46:10; James 1:19.

Sometimes, somewhere we know that without
silence words lose their meaning, that without
listening speaking no longer heals, that without
closeness distance cannot cure.

Henri Nouwen

Spend some time today being still, reflecting over this chapter on social concern, and pray that the Lord may distil all that you have seen, heard, thought, and responded to. Pray for grace and strength to apply the distilled drops of wisdom.

Prayer

Lord, our heavenly Father, whose Son came not to be served but to serve, bless us in our desire and commitment to serve you and others in this world. Give us wisdom, patience and courage to strengthen the weak and raise up those who fall, that being inspired by your love we may minister in your name by word and deed to the suffering, the friendless and the needy; for the sake of your Son, who laid down his life for us, Jesus Christ our Saviour. Amen.

CHAPTER 6

How can we receive power for evangelism?

The story Luke tells in the Acts of the Apostles is exciting and fascinating. It is about real people in real life. It is, in short, the Spirit of God doing his thing in the midst of a world intent on doing its thing. It is about the acts of the Holy Spirit in the acts of the apostles.

There is talk and there is action. There are riots, demonstrations, arrests by the police, shipwreck, unfairness on the part of some public officials and astuteness on the part of others, humour, sarcasm, charges of various kinds with spirited defence, all incidental to the real action threading its way through these events. The thread is evangelism, purely and simply telling the good news of Jesus Christ and depending upon the power of the Spirit to make that good news real to everyone who hears.

Pentecost

The day of Pentecost occupies a significant place in the book of Acts. First, the word 'Pentecost' itself literally means 'fiftieth'. It was the fiftieth day after the Passover—the great moment of Israel's history of deliverance from Egyptian bondage.

In the book of Acts, Pentecost falls fifty days after the great passover of the cross and resurrection, that is, when Jesus was offered as a sacrifice for sin. We therefore cannot understand the significance of Pentecost without the cross, for the coming of the Holy Spirit was to accomplish in us what Jesus Christ had accomplished by his death for us.

> *Repent and be baptized every one of you, in the name of Jesus Christ, for the forgiveness of your sins. And you will receive the gift of the Holy Spirit.*
> Acts 2:38

Pentecost also fulfils the promise of Jesus:

> *You will receive power when the Holy Spirit comes on you.*
> Acts 1:8

Secondly, Pentecost was also a celebration of the giving of the Law (Commandments). But God's ultimate purpose was to write his law on our hearts (Jeremiah 31:33). It is this promise which is being fulfilled at Pentecost.

Why is Pentecost so exciting?

There are several reasons why Pentecost has an exciting application for our own lives.

◆ Penetecost is not only a saving event—it brings the application of the death of Jesus Christ to our lives.

143

◆ It is not only a moral event—it is designed to change our character.

◆ It is also a missionary event!

Pentecost was also called the Feast of First Fruits. It was the time when the first ripe corn was offered to God.

The Pentecost in Acts 2 was to see the first fruits of the harvest of the gospel—and that harvest is still being gathered all over the world today.

What is the Holy Spirit for?

◆ Do we need the Holy Spirit in order to have fellowship?

◆ Do we need the Holy Spirit for worship?

◆ Do we need the Holy Spirit for inner healing?

The Holy Spirit certainly does empower fellowship, worship and inner healing, but when Jesus promises the gift of the Holy Spirit to his disciples, just before his ascension, he says that the direct result of this gift is that the disciples will become his witnesses in Jerusalem, Judea, Samaria and to the ends of the earth.

So when the Spirit came at Pentecost, the disciples became natural evangelists! The Spirit is the moving power, energy, inspiration and strength behind all evangelism.

There are some amazing events in nature which illustrate this point perfectly. I remember once seeing a picture in a magazine which showed a straw that had penetrated an iron light pole during a tornado. I wondered to myself how such a fragile straw could possibly penetrate a light pole? The reason was that the wind which was driving the straw was so powerful that the penetrating force of the straw became absolutely tremendous.

Our Lord Jesus Christ has promised power even greater than that, power that comes from the Holy Spirit. *We do not evangelize alone*. We are not going to 'our Jerusalem' without God's help. The Holy Spirit guides us. The Holy Spirit gives us boldness. The Holy Spirit has given us the Word of God. The Holy Spirit alone can bring conviction and faith. Therefore we are dependent on him, because without the Holy Spirit we labour in vain.

Different kinds of missionaries

There are three types of missionaries in Acts 8, 11 and 13:

◆ Stay-put missionaries, such as the apostles who stayed put in Jerusalem (Acts 8:1).

◆ Share-as-you-go missionaries like Philip and the nameless ones from Cyprus and Cyrene, who gossiped the gospel wherever they went (Acts 8:4)!

◆ Set-apart missionaries like Barnabas and Saul (Acts 13:2).

We need all three types of missionary in the church today. Indeed, there has always been a need for all three types of missionaries for the task has always been immense. The first great piece of news, however, is that the Holy Spirit will guide each of us because he *is* the moving force behind *all* evangelism.

The second great piece of news is that all we have to do to try to find him is to pray—wherever we are—because the Holy Spirit inspires prayer and is released through prayer.

Prayer in our life

One of the important points about natural evangelism is that prayer, more than anything else, should become as natural as breathing. When you're at the bus stop, you can pray. When you're brushing your teeth, or standing at the checkout counter at the supermarket, or waiting at the pedestrian crossing, you can pray. And who said you always have to close your eyes? God is in everyone and in every article of creation around you, and sometimes it's good to *see* in prayer. You can pray silently, or out loud, you can sing or you can whisper... all forms of prayer are acceptable to God when it comes from our deep need for him.

This free attitude to prayer will also help loosen up our worship life. Do you ever find yourself listening to the minister, and agreeing with him in your heart, and then there's a pause and you suddenly stop and look up? Others do, too. Has he lost his place? Is there something wrong?

Aren't we silly! What a waste of valuable prayer time to be so distracted by a pause in the proceedings! The minister is probably lost in prayer himself, and we sometimes need to shake off the tramlines of our expectations, and use every moment we can just to relax into the presence of the Holy Spirit.

Prayer in the New Testament

Prayer is the lifeline of New Testament evangelism, the oxygen for its holy fire. The New Testament was born in prayer. It knows no evangelism without prayer and no prayer which does not lead to evangelism.

Luke's Gospel relates everything to prayer—not that prayer is everything, rather that everything is by prayer. Scene after scene we see Jesus in prayer. Jesus prayed the activity into being, then proceeded to bring about the action.

> *The harvest is plentiful but the workers are few. Pray therefore the Lord of the harvest, to send out workers into his harvest field.*
> **Matthew 9:37–38**

Jesus practised prayer himself, then passed it along to the disciples and he sent them to evangelize—the way that he was evangelizing:

◆ He wanted them to evangelize with the same message.

◆ He wanted them to evangelize with the same power.

◆ He wanted them to evangelize with the same results.

Their going would be as if he were going: 'He who listens to you listens to me' (Luke 10:16).

147

The seventy-one others were sent with the same commission. Today, we are sent out.

Extraordinary results of prayer

There is no good scientific or logical reason why prayer as an activity works. How can it?

Yet it was one of the most important and certainly the most central of all Jesus' activities. Why?

The answer is, of course, neither scientific nor logical—and yet the result of the centrality of prayer is an undeniable fact: for two thousand years there has been a growing awareness of the love of God as shown in the life of his son. And it all began from Jesus' own prayer life, which motivated and multiplied the whole mighty prayer movement.

The secrets learned in Galilee with Jesus were put to work in Jerusalem's famous upper room, as we read in the Book of Acts:

> *They all joined together constantly in prayer,*
> *along with the women and Mary the mother of*
> *Jesus, and with his brothers.*
> **Acts 1:14.**

Again on the day of Pentecost they were all together in one place, almost certainly in prayer, when the Holy Spirit came upon them.

John Wesley said, 'All of God's works are done through believing prayer.'

In his mighty nineteenth-century revivals, Charles Finney increasingly stressed the primacy of prayer. He knew no other way. A man of prayer himself, he would take an intercessor with him when he was invited to a city.

Prayer can do more than launch a spiritual awakening, it can turn out to *be* the awakening.

Jeremiah Lanphier had no idea what could happen when he called for a noonday prayer meeting in New York city on 23 September 1857. Only six people came. They sensed no mighty rushing wind from heaven. However, a movement started which became the mightiest spiritual awakening the United States has yet known.

Within two years, thousands of people had found Jesus Christ—people from every level of society and walk of life. It was the most 'ecumenical' revival in US history, as people from every kind of church, and from no church, met for prayer. Think of it—most of these converts came to Christ in a prayer meeting! It was known as 'the prayer revival'. Compared to other evangelistic meetings it was a flood tide, coming at a desperate period in the nation's history.

Indeed, prayer is so important that D. L. Moody remarked that 'every work of God can be traced to some kneeling form.'

Prayer in worship today

Today, churches which are experiencing revival, such as that experienced in the book of Acts, are characterized by a new surge in prayer life.

John Simons, writing in *Anglicans for Renewal*, shares his experience in Korea where the Yoido

Church has very nearly one million members. What do the growing Christians of Asia do? Answer: they pray... they pray... they pray... and they pray. Their dependence on prayer is overwhelming, and stands in stark profile against the rather casual take-it-or-leave-it attitude in some British prayer meetings.

In fact, at Yoido Church in Korea they have a prayer meeting every night. It lasts for *five hours*—from 10.00 pm to 3.00 am. The average attendance is 1,200 people.

On Friday evening there is the week's main central prayer meeting at which 50,000 Christians participate from 10.00 pm to 3.00 am every week. And the first dawn prayer meeting to follow is underway soon after at 4.30 am (*Anglicans for Renewal*, volume 46).

Curiously enough, this example from Korea shows that the human race has needs today that are no different from those of the apostle Paul, as he pleaded for his churches to engage in prayer for his work.

> *I urge you, by our Lord Jesus Christ, and by the love of the Spirit, to join me in my struggle by praying to God for me.*
> **Romans 15:30**

Reasons for prayer

Why pray? Because it gives the correct perspective on our work. To pray is to say, in effect, I may or may not be capable of clever plans by myself, but these will not guarantee anything; I need God's spirit to go forward in the right way.

Prayer also demonstrates our attitude to all kinds of things—an attitude of confidence in the right guiding principles, principles such as honesty, integrity, growth, fairness and justice. Prayer is one of the spiritual weapons God has given us, and we all know that it is only used weapons that help us in our challenges!

We, too, need to mobilize ourselves into a strong prayer life in order to evangelize. By praying we can all share in the missionary task.

What should be the content of our prayers?

At first sight, we may be rather surprised to study the Bible exhortations for prayer because, unlike our petitionary prayer which seems to be mainly for ourselves, those in the Bible are urged to pray far more for those *taking* the message rather than those listening to the message.

This is because the Bible sees conversion as the work of the Spirit—hence if those who bring the Word of God to people are filled with the Spirit, so God's Spirit is released and opens hardened hearts, deaf ears and blind eyes.

In Luke 4:18, Jesus reads the scroll of the Prophet Isaiah:

The Spirit of the Lord is upon me. He has chosen me to bring good news to the poor, to proclaim freedom for prisoners, and recovery of sight for the blind, to release the oppressed... today this scripture is fulfilled in your hearing.

151

It is because the Spirit is on Jesus that he is able to do this. So the Apostle Paul's exhortations are for prayer for the message takers (1 Timothy 2:1–8). The Lord does not want anyone to perish (2 Peter 3:9). It is the Spirit only which can convict of sin and reveal Jesus (John 16:8–16). No one can say Jesus is Lord except by the Spirit of God. This is why Paul wants people to pray for the evangelists, for unless the Spirit works in his preaching and witness nothing will happen; it must have been a comfort for him to know that... 'if God's word goes out it will not return void' (Isaiah 55:11).

Clearly, the idea of prayer was not new. The Old Testament writers also stressed the need for prayer:

> *Far be it from me that I should sin against the Lord by failing to pray for you.*
> **1 Samuel 12:23**

In the New Testament, Jesus and others expected the church to pray for unbelievers, but hand in hand with this came the exhortation to pray for those who took the gospel message, and for the work of the Spirit in and through them. Paul says:

> *Devote yourselves to prayer, being watchful and thankful. And pray for us, too, that God may open a door for our message, so that we may proclaim the mystery of Christ, for which I am in chains. Pray that I may proclaim it clearly, as I should.*
> **Colossians 4:2–4**

Therefore, we are instructed to pray:

1. For workers to be sent to the mission field (Matthew 9:37–38).

2. For guidance—who to send and where to go (Acts 13:1–3).

3. For the success of the message (Ephesians 6:19–20).

4. For protection and help for missionaries and all who witness (Romans 15:31).

5. For our enemies and persecutors. Jesus leads the way by asking his Father to forgive those who are crucifying him (Luke 23:34). Abraham does this with Sodom and Gomorrah (Genesis 18:16).

The Holy Spirit in prayer

Some people have been given the gift of tongues to pray in the Spirit, but they may use it quite rarely. If you have this gift and want to use it more, just relax—use it in whatever way and whatever times you are guided to do so. Of course, this doesn't give you *carte blanche* to walk into the doctor's waiting room or the Parent Teacher Association AGM and parade your gift as if nothing else mattered. We all need to be sensitive to the real needs of the situation. But it does mean you may have confidence in the Holy Spirit to speak through you when the time is right.

Other people receive promptings from the Holy Spirit when they pray. This doesn't often happen, otherwise all the major disasters in the world might be averted and humankind might arguably lose their free will. But it does mean that if you listen closely to the Spirit, you may hear something important.

A rather funny example of this concerns a friend of mine, Russ, who heard God telling him in a dream to get up and talk to his milkman—at four in the morning! And Russ thought, 'You must be joking!' But God had told him, so he got up and went to the door to wait for his milkman, and I can't tell you what a fool he felt.

When he heard the bottles going down on the doorstep, he opened the door and said hello. Can you imagine?! The milkman nearly fainted! But then the milkman said, 'Hello, Russ.' They knew each other—from school! The milkman's wife had just become a Christian, and he himself had been thinking about Christian things. And Russ said, 'God told me to tell you that he loves you.' And his friend said, 'That's amazing, because this is my last week on the round.'

God prompts us, as he prompted Russ, to *act*. We have to *trust* that he's right *before we can know* he's right—but if we trust, we'll find out he *is* right. In my own experience, God once gave me the name of a man whom he was calling to be an evangelist—the man at that point wasn't even a Christian. It was a name I didn't know, but I was still prompted to give out this information. Afterwards, someone of that name came forward. Curious indeed, by human standards; not at all curious for God!

Such promptings proliferate in the Bible. Not only do they occur frequently in the Old Testament, from the times of Abraham and Moses through Samuel to the later prophets, they continue in the New Testament as well. Paul's first, dramatic exchange with God is one of the most startling, but there are other, gentler stories—for instance, Acts 8:26–40 when an angel of the Lord spoke to Philip.

Philip wasn't one of the original twelve disciples, and it's heart-warming to know that an angel wanted to speak to him. Philip not only sees the angel but he is sufficiently attuned to the Spirit to hear the prompting that instructed him to go to the man in the chariot (verse 29).

The Spirit tells Philip to go to the chariot and stay near it. Now, can you picture Philip? The Spirit of the Lord speaks to him, and Philip's reaction must have been 'Er... what? Are you sure?'

But he, I, you—all of us have got to go if God says things. Philip does what he is told; he takes the first step and God gives him another step and so he takes the second. So many times, we will find the same pattern in these divine appointments: that is, as we continue to respond in obedience, God gives us more information and we can take another step.

It is in this situation that the eunuch professes faith and is baptized. And when they came up out of the water, the Spirit of the Lord certainly took Philip (verse 39)! I imagine when Philip got to the next town he had a lot to talk about!

What about the everyday?

To a degree, the situation Philip found himself in was like our modern-day revivals, where unusual things happen. We should, however, be open to the moving of the Spirit at all times, and there is still a principle in place in Philip's story about being open to being directed by God, regardless of how unlikely we may think it is that we can share our faith. So, are we sure we are available to God in this way?

One of the gifts of the Spirit is the 'word of knowledge'. Nowadays, this word of knowledge refers to some information from the Spirit that can't be gleaned by human means. With it we need, of course, to be bold, but we also need to be spiced with wisdom and sensitivity. It simply won't do to receive supernatural insight and then say, 'By the way, you have just cheated on your husband!'

Jesus could have said this to the Samaritan woman in John 4, but he didn't. Instead he said, 'Go, call your husband.' Maybe we can say, 'Are you having some problems at home?' In this way, if in doubt, we won't stick our foot in it!

The Holy Spirit in church evangelism

In Acts 16, Paul and his team had been experiencing frustration after frustration. Doors were closing against them rather than opening, confounding their plans rather than fulfilling them. But it was the work of the Holy Spirit. They had to learn to die to their own plans for the sake of God's plans, to die to their own timetable in order to live by God's. Through a wonderful dream, they were directed to go to Macedonia and God opened up an amazing new door into Europe (Acts 16:1–15).

Of course, this story does not mean that God does not want us to have plans. But there must be room for divine initiative. It is the experience of a number of churches that they find that there are some areas in their communities which are often more receptive to the gospel than others. Clearly we shouldn't stop evangelizing anywhere, but we would do well to wait on the Spirit for him to show us where he wants us to concentrate our evangelistic efforts—it may be a geographical region, or it may be a certain sector of the community—the children, the elderly, the single parents, the ethnic minorities, and so on.

The question for you and me, therefore, is this: where is the Spirit moving over the face of the waters to prepare for life to spring forth?

The Holy Spirit in witnessing with words and deeds

When Jesus sent out his first missionary teams:

> *He gave them power and authority to drive out all demons and to cure diseases, and he sent them to preach the kingdom of God and to heal the sick.*
> **Luke 9:1**

It was therefore natural for the disciples to continue this kind of evangelism (Acts 3:1–10; 19:11–16). God loves the world so much that he wants to bring his healing and deliverance.

The Holy Spirit in spiritual warfare

The Spirit helps us to understand the spiritual warfare, and to see things as God sees them.

It is not a pleasant fact, but over 150 magazines about the occult are available in Britain, and one in four spiritual books published each year is about the occult. But one of the great qualities about the release of the Spirit, as prophesied in Joel 2:28, is that it is characterized by a release of prophecy and vision. In other words, the Holy Spirit promises that he will help us to see things from heaven's point of view.

In recent years the church in the West has increasingly had to face up to the critical issues of understanding the biblical terms 'principalities and powers' and of knowing how effectively to engage them in spiritual warfare. As an example of the challenge, think about the following words written in the foreword to a fascinating study by Thomas H. McAlpine, *Facing the Powers*, published by MARC:

All over the world, folk in missions are beginning to recognize that the biblical language about principalities and powers cannot be dismissed as first-century, pre-scientific superstition. The world of spirits and the supernatural is real and has its impact on mission. Sadly, we in the West are ill-equipped to think with clarity and depth because our dominant Enlightenment paradigm has no space for this level of reality.

Paul tells us that Satan has blinded the mind of the unbeliever, so every action of bringing someone to Christ involves the battle.

There were also times when Satan succeeded in preventing even the apostle Paul from carrying out his own missionary travels (1 Thessalonians 2:18), so we should not be surprised if we meet with opposition in our evangelism.

But if we do allow the Holy Spirit to permeate our lives completely, it is amazing what he can do. Paul Yongii Cho in Korea says the church has grown so fast because 'we have learned to clear the skies.'

Further evidence of this is given by one of the most effective evangelists today, the Argentinian Carlos Anacondia. Dr Peter Wagner, a church growth specialist, has done some research into Anacondia's evangelism, asking why it is so fruitful, and he writes:

Because of Anacondia's intentional, premeditated, high energy approach to spiritual warfare, he also skillfully contextualizes his message and methodology to communicate with and meet the needs of the lower classes. One of his discoveries is the efficacy of power and evangelism and spiritual warfare for that particular audience.

Spiritual Power in Urban Evangelism

Summary

The Acts of the Apostles is all about evangelism, but it does not sanctify any certain method of evangelism.

Every conceivable way is employed by the apostles to tell the good news of Jesus Christ.

All of us are human. The apostles were human. Luke makes that quite clear. He also makes it clear that people such as ourselves can tell the good news of Jesus Christ in the power of the Spirit. We therefore need to have the openness of the Spirit to move powerfully among us if we are to be effective in our evangelism. This way, the Holy Spirit of God reveals Jesus, through us, to the world.

Therefore, we need the Holy Spirit:

◆ to inspire our prayer;

◆ for direction in personal and church evangelism;

◆ for witnessing with signs and wonders;

◆ for spiritual warfare.

Prayer

Almighty God, our Father, you have redeemed us by the death and resurrection of your Son Jesus Christ and given us your Holy Spirit that we may be your witnesses in the world: banish the powers of darkness and sin from the minds of those who do not believe in your name and open their hearts to your gospel that they may believe in you and become temples of your Holy Spirit. Grant also that we who believe in you may be effective servants of your word to those whose lives have not been touched by your saving grace. We make this prayer through our Lord Jesus Christ who reigns with you and the Holy Spirit, one God forever and ever. Amen.

Yoido church, Korea

Exercise One

Take a moment to reflect on your church and personal prayer life. Can any changes and improvements be made to develop prayer in relation to evangelism? Jot these down.

Exercise Two

Think about the area your church serves. Where has the gospel been well received (socially and geographically)? Where are the barren places? After thinking about this, spend some time listening to the Lord and see if you sense the Spirit of God directing you to evangelize in a particular region or section of your community. If you have a strong sense of God speaking about a particular area, write down your thoughts and then commit yourself to asking your church leadership how you can proceed.

End this exercise by praying for the barren places that you have become aware of.

Renew thy wonders in this our day as by a new Pentecost.

Pope John XXIII

161

Exercise Three

This is the last exercise of the course!

Ask that the Holy Spirit would come to you with power and boldness for evangelism. If you are not sure what to pray, here is a prayer you could use which is based on Acts 4:29–30.

> *Father in heaven,*
> *thank you that you have given us the*
> *wonderful gift of your Holy Spirit.*
> *Send now your Spirit on me.*
> *Enable me to speak your word with great*
> *boldness.*
> *Stretch out your hand to work through me*
> *signs and wonders in the name of your holy*
> *servant Jesus,*
> *that many may experience your power and*
> *your love through me. Amen.*

Remain quiet for a while, allowing the Spirit to work. Ask God to give you prophetic words and pictures to encourage you. Open your heart in faith, believing that God is working powerfully in your life.

Daily Studies

Day one

Read Acts 1:14, 2:42 and 6:1–7.

In Acts 1, the apostles, Mary the mother of Jesus and some others devoted themselves to prayer. In Acts 2, the

3,000 new Christians devoted themselves to the apostles' teaching, fellowship, breaking of bread and prayer.

In Acts 6, the apostles devoted themselves to prayer and the ministry of the word.

> *The word 'devoted' means 'intensely enthusiastic, ardent, dedicated and consecrated'. Pray today that the Holy Spirit will help your will to be devoted and dedicated to have communion with the Lord. Fear not because your prayer is stammering, your words feeble and your language poor. Jesus can understand you.*
>
> **J. C. L. Ryle**

> *When we pray, the simpler our prayers are the better; the plainest, humblest language which expresses our meaning is best.*
>
> **Charles Spurgeon**

Prayer

> *Thank God for his Spirit, and pray that he will continue to fill you for evangelism.*

Day two

Read Acts 4:23–31.

Peter and John have just been interrogated by a group of very powerful and distinguished Jewish leaders. Most people would be greatly intimidated by this, but John and Peter both find that in this situation they are given great boldness and wisdom. On their return, despite knowing the storm clouds are gathering, they pray for a further release of the Spirit.

Take a look at this prayer. What do you learn about prayer from it? Where do you think God wants you to speak for him with boldness? Ask him about this today.

Think again about the people whose names you wrote down in Chapter 3. Is there going to be an opportunity to speak boldly to any of them today? Pray for them again.

Prayer

Father, I am weak, but you are strong.
I have no words, but you sent your Son who
is the Word.
I have no love, but you sent your Spirit who
pours your love into our hearts.
Come touch me today:
fill me afresh with the life-giving Spirit
and use me today in compassion and
boldness to tell others about your Son, Jesus,
that the rivers of life may flow from my heart
to others. Amen.

Day three

Read Ephesians 5:15–20.

What does it mean to be filled with the Holy Spirit? Simply, it means being like Jesus. When you are filled with the Holy Spirit, the risen Christ in all of his mighty powerful presence lives in your body, thinks with your mind, loves with your heart, and speaks with your lips. And since he came to seek and save the lost, he walks around in your body, seeking and saving the lost.

Being filled with the Holy Spirit means, according to John 15:7, to abide in Christ. That is what the Christian life is all about—walking day by day in the fullness and joy and the power and adventure of the third person of the Trinity, God the Holy Spirit. As a result, God the Son will be exalted and honoured and worshipped and praised and adored. That is the role of the Holy Spirit. He did not come to glorify himself.

Pray that we may discover a fresh experience of being filled with the Spirit today, so that Jesus will be glorified.

Prayer

Give us now, O merciful Father, thy Holy Spirit, that we may be strengthened for the work of this day, through Jesus Christ thy Son, our Lord. Amen.

Day four

Read 1 Corinthians 13.

This is probably one of the most famous passages in the Bible. Try to imagine that you are reading this passage for the first time, and allow God to speak to you through it.

God is love, so you could substitute 'God' for 'love' in verse 4 which gives you an insight into the character of God.

> *For God so loved the world that he gave his one and only Son, that whoever believes in him shall not perish but have eternal life.*
> John 3:16

God's love is expressed towards the lost world, and such is the extent of his love that he sends his beloved Son to rescue us.

Let the Spirit explore your heart today. Are there any hard places that need softening? Is there any forgiving that needs to be done? Give some thought to your relationships with friends who do not go to church, especially those you wrote about in Chapter 3.

Do you love them, full-stop? Or only to some extent, on certain conditions? Do you love unconditionally? Or only when they behave a certain way towards you (politely, for instance, or punctually or soberly)—are you in fact extracting a kind of *payment* from them for your relationship with them? (Your behaviour might imply, for instance, ' You will be courteous and on time when dealing with me, or else I will be distant towards you and withhold my affection.')

It is hard to do, but if you really want to be concerned for their spiritual well-being now, and their eternal destiny, you must love without 'payment'. Evangelism without unconditional love will become cold and clinical—a practised art of rhetoric and calculated exhortation. But where your heart is alight with the fire of God for a person, then the Spirit of God can stir and set light to that person's life. Pray for the Spirit to come and stir up love in your heart again, no matter what their failings—or yours!

Meditate on this verse.

God has poured out his love into our hearts by the Holy Spirit, whom he has given us.
Romans 5:5

Prayer

Use a personalized version of the verse from Romans as a repetitive prayer, saying it once, then pausing and repeating it. As you do this, be aware of the Spirit of God filling you with God's love. Repeat this several times until you sense God's filling is complete.

Lord God, pour your love into my heart through the Holy Spirit whom you have given me.

Now, with the love of God in your heart, pray for those you wrote about earlier.

Day five

Read Matthew 24:1–14.

God has a master plan for this universe:

It is not for you to know the times or dates the Father has set by his own authority.
Acts 1:7

Christ is coming again—he said so himself:

> *In my Father's house are many rooms; if it were not so, I would have told you. I am going there to prepare a place for you. And if I go and prepare a place for you, I will come back and take you to be with me that you also may be where I am.*
> John 14:2–3

Read Matthew 26:63–64.

What is the purpose of his second coming? The Bible tells us:

◆ Christ is coming to judge (Acts 17:31; 2 Timothy 4:1).

◆ Christ is coming to reign (1 Corinthians 15:24–28; Revelation 11:15).

When we participate in the rich symbolism of the Lord's Supper, we have before us our motivation, our message and our marching orders. It is a missionary meal.

In the broken bread and poured-out wine, we have a powerful reminder of the price God paid for our liberation from the power and penalty of sin, and a compelling reason why we must now be totally dedicated to him and his service.

He died for all, that those who live should no longer live for themselves but for him who died for them and was raised again.

Pray to God to give you such a vision of the second coming that you will gladly labour in the harvest field until he comes.

Therefore, my dear friends, stand firm. Let nothing move you. Always give yourselves fully to the work of the Lord, because you know that your labour in the Lord is not in vain.

1 Corinthians 15:58

Prayer

Lord, the task is not finished; keep me pressing forward, help me to be a faithful servant and witness of yours till we meet in glory. Amen.

Day six

This is the last daily reading in *Natural Evangelism*. Think today about the six weeks this course has covered, and look through your notebook.

- ◆ What were the parts which meant a lot to you and which you will treasure?
- ◆ In what ways, if at all, has your approach to evangelism changed?
- ◆ Which passage from the Bible meant most to you? Turn to it and read it again.

Now take a few moments to think out and complete in your notebook the following sentence, which will be your commitment to ongoing friendship evangelism.

This is between you and the Lord. Take a moment to pray about your commitment, then write it out after the following beginning:

Following this course I commit myself to: ....
....
....
....

Now that it is written down, take a look at it and pray about it again. If you find yourself doubting your own commitment, read 1 Corinthians 15:58.

Finally, pray for your friends and neighbours whose names you wrote down earlier, and work out how you are going to continue to pray for them and evangelize to them in the weeks to come. You might like to try the Singapore '5-3-1' method, which is:

◆ Prayerfully seek the Lord for five friends who have yet to meet Christ (select their names from your writing) and commit yourself to praying for them regularly for a year.

◆ Ask God that by the end of the year you will have had the opportunity to speak to at least three of them about Christ.

◆ Pray that by the end of the year at least one of them has come to Christ—*whether or not* you personally are aware of it.

If everyone were to do this successfully, every church would double its size every year!

Final Prayer

Heavenly Father, thank you for sending your Son, Jesus Christ, into the world to save sinners.
Thank you for sending us your Holy Spirit to empower me to tell others about Christ.
Thank you for all that I have learned in this book.
Thank you for giving me the strength to make a commitment.
Help me to remember, at all times, that you are with me; and that it is your will I must do—not my own.
Now send me out in the power of the Spirit, that I may live out all that I have learned.
In the name of Jesus Christ my Lord. Amen.

Conclusion

I do very much hope you've enjoyed this course. The main thing, as they say, is to keep the main thing the main thing (say it out loud and you'll get it!) which is:

to know Christ and make him known.

God had one Son and he was a missionary. We need to follow him effectively rather than efficiently—efficiency is doing things right; effectiveness is doing right things. Therefore let our evangelism be:

1. **Continuous: let it go on all the time (Acts 2:47).**

2. **Congregational: let the whole church be mobilized (John 20:21).**

3. **Caring: let it be demonstrated by love and sensitivity to people's needs (1 Thessalonians 2:7–8).**

4. **Conserving: let each new believer grow spiritually and become active (Colossians 1:28–29).**

If you are still wondering if the course has been successful for you—well, have you heard God? If you have, will you obey? If so, it has been successful! A friend of mine, Leighton Ford, wrote:

Jesus was born in a borrowed manger. He preached from a borrowed boat. He entered

Jerusalem on a borrowed donkey. He ate the Last Supper in a borrowed upper room and he was buried in a borrowed tomb. Now he asks to borrow the lives of Christians to reach the rest of the world. If we do not speak, then he is dumb and silent.

Amen, Lord Jesus, Amen!

Notes